CW00569942

KS1 & KS2

School Assembly Resource Book

by
Sue Garnett

Published by
Topical Resources

This book contains: 34 original stories; 24 original poems;
6 short plays and is accompanied by a FREE CD ROM
to enable you to:

Project full-colour illustrations for each story
using an O.H.P. or Data Projector
Project text for each poem for reference or choral speaking
Print out scripts for each short play.

Topical Resources publishes a range of Educational Materials for use in Primary Schools and Pre-School Nurseries and Playgroups.

For the latest catalogue:
Tel. 01772 863158
Fax. 01772 866153
e.mail: sales@topical-resources.co.uk
Visit our website at: www.topical-resources.co.uk

Copyright © 2002 Sue Garnett
Illustrated by John Hutchinson

Typeset by Art Works,
Fairhaven, 69 Worden Lane, Leyland, Preston PR25 3BD

Printed in Great Britain for 'Topical Resources',
Publishes of Educational Materials, P.O. Box 329, Broughton,
Preston, Lancashire PR3 5LT by
T.Snape & Company Limited, Bolton's Court, Preston,
Lancashire.

First Published January 2002

ISBN 1 872977 65 0

Introduction

Sue Garnett has been a Lancashire Headteacher for over eight years. Her desire to use a variety of approaches whilst leading school assemblies has led to the production of this unique KS1 & KS2 resource book and accompanying CD ROM.

The book contains 34 original stories, 24 original poems and 6 short plays gathered together in themes, which are common to most primary schools. These are: Harvest, Christmas, New Year, Easter, Wonderful World, Magic, All Kinds of Children, Consequences, Anger, Honesty, Greed and Love.

Each story, poem or play found in the book has an accompanying CD ROM reference to help find additional resources to the printed page.

Each story in the book has a small line drawing to illustrate the account. Larger, full colour versions of these line drawings can be found on the CD ROM by looking up the appropriate CD ROM reference.

The pictures are stored as Jpeg files. These can be opened within any suitable image handling software, such as Adobe PhotoDeluxe, or the Microsoft Imaging Accessory. They can also be veiwed and printed from within Microsoft Word. (Go to: Insert / Picture / From File).

Using a Data Projector, these images can be used to help illustrate the story during the delivery of the school assembly. If a Data Projector is not available, the images can be printed on to appropriate easily available transparency films using an ink jet printer. These transparencies can then be used in the normal way on an Overhead Projector. Examples of some of the colour images can be found on the back cover of this book.

The complete text of each poem in the book can also be found on the CD ROM by looking up the appropriate reference. These too can be projected during the school assembly and used for reference or choral speaking.

The six short plays in the book can also be found on the CD ROM by looking up the appropriate reference. Multiple copies of each script may then be printed out for small groups of children to practise with before performing to the rest of the school.

Contents

Contents

HARVEST 1

Harvest is a wonderful time of year when we can appreciate all the gifts God has given us. In particular it should make us think of people less fortunate than ourselves. This story is about a boy who gives a lonely old man a harvest.

 Illustration available on CD ROM   ref: 01

The Harvest Gift

The children at St. Paul's school were practising for the harvest service. They were given letters to take home. David noticed the tear off slip at the bottom where you had to write the name of someone who would like a harvest gift. This person had to be old, sick or living on his/her own. David couldn't think of anyone.

When he got home there was no one in so he decided to go for a ride on his bike. He got changed into his jeans and took his bike out of the shed. It was a beautiful day, just right for a bike ride. He cycled down the street and up the lane towards the woods. He stopped when he came to the stream, jumped off his bike and picked up a few stones. He threw them into the water.

Along the side of the stream was an overgrown track just wide enough for a small car. He'd never been down the track before and wondered where it went. He decided to explore. It was very bumpy and the wheels on his racing bike wobbled. The sun was sinking fast and it cast strange shadows. David shivered but rode on until the track came to a dead end. He could see smoke rising through the trees. David got off his bike and wheeled it into the clearing. There in front of him was a cottage with smoke coming out of the chimney. The front door of the cottage was open and there was a rocking chair on the veranda. An old man was sitting on the chair smoking a pipe.

"Hello" said the man in a friendly tone. "What can I do for you?"

"Oh!" said David, quite surprised. "I was just having a ride."

"What's your name?" asked the old man.

"David," he replied, walking up the garden path.

"Ah, you're young David Fisher, aren't you?" said the old man. "I knew your grandfather. We were good friends."

The old man told him about his wife who had died over five years ago. David noticed the walking stick by his side and his shaky hands. He wondered who did the old man's shopping and repairs to his house, and who talked to him when he was feeling down. They had been chatting for quite a

while when David noticed the time.

"Oh no!" he shouted, "It's nearly five o'clock. I'll have to go."

"Come back again soon," said the old man, "and don't forget to tell your parents where you've been."

David did forget to tell his parents about the old man. School was so busy there was no time to think about anything else but the harvest service. There were practices at playtimes, practices in the afternoon and practices at home time. David didn't seem to have a moment's rest. Then it was Sunday and the harvest service.

The church looked wonderful. Everybody smiled when the youngest children walked up the aisle dressed as fruit and vegetables. Some of the

smaller ones waved to their parents and then the one dressed as a pineapple tripped up. Her pineapple hat fell off and rolled down the aisle. The little girl chased after it and the other infants giggled.

After the service David watched the adults putting all the harvest gifts into their car boots and then walked home with his parents. When they were eating lunch, David told his parents all about the old man.

"He's not on the list for receiving a gift. He's no family. He's all alone," said David. "We've got to do something."

"Well I made some bread this morning," said Mum. "It's only just come out of the oven but I'm sure it would taste delicious with some plum jam."

"Brilliant," said David, "but … I finished off the last spoonful of jam on my toast this morning."

"Don't worry about that," said Dad. "Mrs Brown called this morning and brought us another jar of her home made plum jam. We could take him a jar of that if you like."

"And I picked some blackberries yesterday. He can have some of those," said Mum.

"But what can I do?" asked David.

"You can fetch the rest of the apples that have fallen from the tree and I'll make an apple pie," said Mum.

"What a great idea," agreed David.

Just two hours later, David and his parents were driving down the track towards the old man's cottage. They could see the old man sitting on the veranda. David leapt out the car and ran up the path, the harvest basket in his hand.

"I've brought you some visitors," David shouted.

The old man woke with a start. His eyes sparkled and he smiled.

"Happy harvest," shouted David cheerfully, giving him the basket.

The old man lifted the cloth and peered into the basket. There was a punnet of blackberries; black and juicy, a fresh brown loaf, a jar of plum jam and a warm apple pie.

"What a lovely surprise," he smiled. "I can't thank you enough."

"It was the least we could do," said David's father holding out his hand in friendship. "After all, it is harvest time."

HARVEST 2

'Farmer Rabbit' tells the story of the Sower from the Bible. It tells Christians how to live their lives in a language that young children can understand.

 Illustration available on CD ROM   ref: 02

Farmer Rabbit

It was harvest time in Rabbit Land. Mr Rabbit was busy bringing in the crops. Mr Rabbit's children usually helped him, but this year they had measles. Peter, Raymond and Georgina Rabbit stood at the door watching their father at work.

"Can we go outside and help father?" asked Peter when they went back in the house.

"No," said Mrs Rabbit. "Finish your homework."

"But I can't do it," said Peter.

"Try harder," said Mrs Rabbit.

"But I can't," said Peter, slamming the book down on the table.

He walked over to the fire where his sister was playing with a jigsaw.

"Can I help you?" he asked.

"No, go away," replied Georgina.

"Oh, please?" begged Peter.

"No." said Georgina in a cross voice.

"Let him play," said Mrs Rabbit.

"No," said Georgina, picking up the jigsaw and taking it into her bedroom. "It's mine."

Suddenly there was a crash. Mrs Rabbit looked over to the window. One of the ornaments had fallen, from the windowsill, onto the floor below. It had broken into many pieces.

"Raymond, I've told you again and again not to play with your toy cars on the windowsill. Now take them off, otherwise you'll break all the ornaments," she said.

"Yes mother," replied Raymond, but really taking no notice.

Mrs Rabbit went back to her ironing. Ten minutes later she heard another crash. She looked over to the window. Another ornament had been broken. Raymond looked over to her.

"Sorry Mum," he said timidly.

"I must have told you three or four times today to take your cars off the windowsill. Now do as you are told."

Mrs Rabbit kept her patience all day, even when Raymond broke another ornament. However, she was glad when Mr Rabbit came home.

"Have you been good today?" asked Mr Rabbit.

The young rabbits looked down at the floor.

"Oh dear," said Mr Rabbit. "You've been naughty haven't you?"

The children nodded.

"You're just like the seeds I planted this spring." said Mr Rabbit sitting down in his comfortable armchair by the fire and gathering the children around him.

"This story is about Farmer Rabbit. He lived just over the hill near the big wood. Well, it was springtime and Farmer Rabbit was busy. There was so much to do in the fields. Farmer Rabbit went to market and bought a packet of lettuce seeds.

"I can't wait for summer," said Farmer Rabbit. "I should have a good crop of juicy lettuce."

The next morning he got up early. He went out into the field to sow the seeds. Just as he was about to begin, he heard a voice. It was his friend, Long Ears.

"Hello Long Ears," said Farmer Rabbit, "Where are you going?"

"I'm going to Lucy Rabbit's birthday party," said Long Ears. "There'll be lots of juicy carrots to eat. Are you coming?"

"No, I'm too busy," said Farmer Rabbit. "I've got a lot of planting to do."

"Never mind," said Long Ears and went on his way.

Farmer Rabbit sighed.

"If I plant these seeds quickly I can

still go to the party," he thought.

He took a handful of seeds out of the bag and set about his work. In no time at all Farmer Rabbit had finished and went off happily to the party.

Farmer Rabbit looked after his seeds all through spring. In the summer he went out to his field to see if his crop was ready.

"Oh dear," he said, looking at the bare field. "What's happened?"

Then he remembered. He had been in such a rush to plant the seeds that some of them had fallen by the wayside and been eaten by animals or trodden on.

"Oh no!" he cried. Then he remembered that some of the seeds had fallen on stony ground. He hadn't bothered to pick them up and put them in the soil. The sun had come up and because there was no soil to keep them moist, they had got scorched and withered away.

"Oh no!" he cried.

Then he remembered that some of the seeds had fallen among the thorns. The thorns had grown around the seeds and choked them.

"Oh no!" he cried.

He was just about to go back to his house when he noticed a few lettuces in the middle of the field. Thank goodness, some of the seeds had fallen on good ground. They had grown into strong healthy plants.

"What does all this mean?" asked the young rabbits.

"The seeds are like people," said Mr Rabbit. "Do you remember the seeds which fell by the wayside? Well those seeds are like people who hear but don't really take any notice."

"A bit like me sometimes," said Raymond, remembering how his mother had told him lots of times not to play with cars on the windowsill and he hadn't listened.

"And the seeds which fell on stony ground and died," said Mr Rabbit, "are like people who listen to God for a while, but as soon as they get into difficulty, because they have no firm belief, they turn away."

"I suppose that's like me with my homework," said Peter. "I give up rather easily."

"And the seeds which fell amongst the thorns and choked," said Mr Rabbit, "are like people who only care for themselves."

"Oh dear," said Georgina Rabbit, beginning to cry, "that's just like me sometimes. I never share things. I only think of myself."

Mr Rabbit put a comforting arm around her shoulder.

"But the seeds which fell on good ground and multiplied are like people with good honest hearts," said Mr Rabbit. "They listen to God's word.

They are kind and love one another, just like your mother. This is what the story means. Now do you understand?"

The children nodded their heads.

"I hope we can be like the seeds which fell on good ground," said the children.

Farmer Rabbit looked at his wife and winked.

"I'm sure you can," he said smiling.

HARVEST 3

At harvest time Christians thank God for all that he has given them. Sometimes they take a gift to church. It doesn't matter how big or small the gift is, it is the thought that counts and the effort that has gone into bringing it. 'The Harvest Basket' tells us the story of a girl who didn't have a gift to take to the harvest service at her local church.

 Illustration available on CD ROM   ref: 03

The Harvest Basket

Rebecca was a quiet girl. She didn't have many friends. Some of the children called her names, especially Donna and a few others. One day after school they found Rebecca alone in the cloakroom.

"Are you coming to the harvest service on Sunday?" asked Donna.

"Perhaps," said Rebecca putting her coat on quickly.

"You've got to bring a harvest basket," said Donna.

"Oh," said Rebecca, "I don't think I'll be able to come after all. I've got to look after my little brothers"

"But you've got to come," said Donna. "Mrs Bennett will be cross if you don't."

The other girls nodded their heads in agreement.

Mrs Bennett was their teacher. Rebecca liked her very much.

"Well, I'll be coming then," said Rebecca.

"Don't forget your harvest basket," said Donna.

"No I won't forget," said Rebecca.

"See you on Sunday then," said Donna.

The girls laughed as they watched Rebecca run across the yard in her tatty coat.

"I bet she won't come," said Donna.

"She hasn't got a harvest basket."

On Saturday morning Rebecca asked her mum if she could go to the harvest service.

"I suppose so," said her mother, "but you'll have to take your brothers too."

"And could I take a harvest basket?" asked Rebecca.

"I'm sorry love, we can't afford one," said Rebecca's mother.

"But Mum," said Rebecca, "everyone else is taking a basket."

"Well you'll just have to go without one this year. Maybe next year. Now go and play."

Rebecca set off down the street. She had to get a basket of fruit. Who else could help? She sat down on a wall to think.

"Hello," said a voice.

It was Mr Barnes, the lollipop man from school.

"Hello," said Rebecca.

Mr Barnes was pushing a wheelbarrow.

"Where are you going?" she asked.

"To my allotment," he said.

"What's that?" asked Rebecca.

"It's a piece of land where I grow things."

"Can I come?" asked Rebecca.

"Of course you can, but ask your mum first," replied Mr Barnes.

Rebecca ran home to ask her mother, who said 'yes' right away. When Rebecca got to the allotment she told Mr Barnes about the harvest basket.

"Maybe I can help you," he said smiling.

Mr Barnes' allotment was fantastic. There were so many plants that Rebecca couldn't name them all. He even had some fruit trees.

Mr Barnes gave Rebecca a small fork.

"You can help me with the weeding," he said.

Rebecca got on with the job. She sang while she worked.

"Time for a drink," said Mr Barnes walking over to his shed.

He heated the water on a gas stove and made some tea. She had two biscuits from the tin. Then they got back to work. Rebecca picked up the weeds and put them on the compost heap.

"I think it's time you were going home," said Mr Barnes.

Rebecca went to the shed to get her coat.

"Haven't you forgotten something?" asked Mr Barnes.

Rebecca looked puzzled.

"I thought you needed a harvest basket for church?"

"I do," said Rebecca.

"Come with me. Let's see what we can do."

Mr Barnes picked up an empty basket. He wiped it out with a cloth and put a clean tea towel inside it. Carefully he picked some plums from the tree and put them in the basket. Then he got a couple of rosy red apples and some pears. Soon the basket was full of fruit.

"This is for you," said Mr Barnes, giving the basket to Rebecca.

"For me?" asked Rebecca, a big smile on her face.

Mr Barnes nodded.

"You deserve it," he said. "You've worked very hard."

Rebecca thanked Mr Barnes and ran off home to show her mum. On Sunday morning she washed her hands and face, put on her uniform and cleaned her shoes until they shone. She found a ribbon to put around the basket.

When she got to church the bells were ringing. The other children stood and stared as Rebecca appeared at the door with the magnificent basket of fruit. She lifted her head high and smiled at them as she walked down the aisle. Carefully she put the basket on the altar steps then took her place with the rest of the children, the proudest girl in the whole school.

HARVEST 4

At harvest time children often enjoy bringing baskets of fruit and vegetables to school or church and delight in seeing the church decorated with produce. The story 'The Harvest Mouse', brings alive the joys of the Harvest Festival and also encourages children to think about home and the importance of families.

 Illustration available on CD ROM   ref: 04

The Harvest Mouse

In the corner of St. James' church, behind the organ, lived a family of mice. In the spring of one particular year Mrs Mouse had two lovely children, Harry and Susie. For the first few weeks they lay quietly in the nest but very soon they were able to run about the church exploring all the nooks and crannies.

Harry and Susie were very happy. They had fun together running up and down the aisles, chasing each other's tails and jumping from pew to pew, but they always remembered their mother's warning,

"When you hear the sound of music from the church organ, you must come straight back to the nest."

"But why?" asked the children.

"I will show you why tomorrow," she

15

replied.

The following morning, the children were very excited. Very early, before the sun had risen in the sky, the whole family scampered to the back of the church and hid under the curtain by the vestry door. They waited in silence until suddenly they heard the sound of bells ringing a happy tune. From behind the curtains the mice watched people hurrying into the church. Then the music began. The young mice listened to the beautiful tunes coming from the organ. They listened to the choir singing and the congregation joining in.

"This is terrific," said the children together, "but why do we have to come back to the nest when we hear the music?"

"It's not safe to play in the church when the humans are around, their feet could trample all over you," said their mother.

And after watching their first service, they always remembered the rule that their mother had taught them and always returned to their nest when they heard the sound of the organ.

Every Sunday the mice took up their positions at the back of the church to listen to the service. Within weeks they were joining in with the hymns and enjoying every minute. But one of the young harvest mice longed for excitement and new experiences. This was Harry. Sly Fox had told him stories about the big city and how wonderful it was. And although Harry's father had told him that it was a dangerous place, Harry didn't believe him.

One night, Harry couldn't sleep a wink and lay tossing and turning in his bed. He decided to get up and climbed out of the nest and went out into the moonlight. "I wonder what lies out there in that big world? I've never been further than the church yard and Farmer Brown's field," he sighed. "I think I'll go and seek my fortune in the big city. I've heard so much about it from Sly Fox. There's so much to do there and so much excitement." Hurriedly Harry scribbled a note for his family and set off. By morning he had arrived in the big city. The noise of the traffic frightened him. There was the honking of horns and engines revving wildly. By a whisker he just missed being run over by a big red bus and dashed onto the pavement for safety, but there was no safety there. He could hear the noise of thudding feet all around him. People of all different shapes and sizes rushed by. Harry ran in and out of them trying to avoid being crushed.

At last he found some peace and quiet in the safety of a side street and lay down to rest. Suddenly he heard a hissing sound. Slowly making its way down the street towards him he could see the shadow of a tall animal with an arched back. The harvest mouse lay very still his heart pounding, hoping the cat wouldn't see him. However the cat had seen him.

"Ha, ha," said the cat, with a wicked glint in his eye, "A harvest mouse. A fat, tasty harvest mouse. Just what I've been looking forward to all day."

In a flash the cat pounced. The harvest mouse ran like the wind down the street. He didn't stop running until he saw Farmer Brown's field.

But what a shock he had. The field was so different. The tall golden corn he had played in was gone and the ground was burned and bare.

"What's happened?" he said. "Owl, Hedgehog, Swallow, Squirrel, Rabbit and Frog, where are you?"

But no one answered. Sadly he crept into a hole, frightened and alone.

"I've been such a selfish mouse," he said, "It's no wonder they've left me."

He climbed out of the hole and scampered along the path to the front door of the church. The door was closing, but with a mighty leap he squeezed through just before the door slammed shut. He made his way to the familiar spot where his family would sit on Sundays.

"Perhaps if I say a little prayer, I might be forgiven for leaving home," he thought.

He shut his eyes tightly. Then something wonderful happened. He heard the sound of the organ and then the sound of scampering feet coming from under the curtain.

"Mum, Dad, Susie, I thought I'd lost you. I'm sorry, I'm really sorry," said Harry with a tremor in his voice.

"Don't worry little one, you're home now and you're safe," said his mother with tears in her eyes.

"You thought that the city would be exciting, but it's a dangerous place for a harvest mouse. You belong here with us," said his father.

"Today is a special day," said his sister Susie. "It's harvest and all our country friends have come to the church with us to say thank you for all the wonders we have been given."

The young harvest mouse looked around him. Owl, Hedgehog, Swallow, Squirrel, Rabbit and Frog were all there with their families.

"And now for something special, much more wonderful than the city," said his mother.

She lifted the curtain just a little. There before him was the most beautiful sight Harry had ever seen in his whole life. The church was so beautiful. Flowers of every colour were arranged around the pews and the windowsills. Baskets of fruit stood by the pulpit and fat, juicy vegetables lay in boxes, almost over-flowing. He could smell freshly baked bread. This was so wonderful.

Then the choir stood up smartly in their starched white surplices. The congregation rose to its feet to sing hymns of praise. The animal folk lifted their heads and smiled at one another. Harry turned to his family and smiled.

"How could I ever have doubted that this wasn't the best place to be!" he said.

"It's wonderful to have you back," his mother sighed. "Happy harvest everyone!"

HARVEST 5

Harvest can be one of the most exciting and creative times of the year. It is a joyful time when for Christians, God's promise of seedtime leading to a good harvest comes true. However it is also a time when Christians think of their responsibility towards the world God created. This play enables the children to understand the need for Conservation, so that we will continue to have harvests for years to come.

(Six children hold up the letters one by one and read out the information for each letter)

 Play Script available on CD ROM refs: 05

Starve

Child 1

S is for the sea.

The sea is polluted. Agricultural and industrial waste, sewage and oil are all polluting the sea.

Child 2

T is for the trees.

Trees in the tropical rainforests are being chopped down to make furniture and houses. They are also cut down to provide space to graze animals and grow crops. Losing the rainforest causes many problems. People and animals lose their homes. Some animals and plants have become extinct. When the trees are removed, the soil sometimes gets washed away in heavy rain and then the land is fit for nothing. The tropical rainforests also play a large part in the world's climate.

Child 3

A is for animals.

Many species of animals have become endangered. Poachers have been killing elephants for their tusks and shooting rhinos for their horns. Fishermen kill seals and their fur is used to make coats. Leopards are also killed for their fur. Fishermen needlessly kill whales and dolphins. Trophy hunters poach mountain gorillas. Chimpanzees are sold to laboratories and holiday photographers in seaside resorts abroad. If we aren't careful these animals will become extinct.

Child 4

R is for the rivers.

Some factories dump chemicals and industrial waste into rivers each day and sewage spills into the rivers. The water isn't fit for drinking and children can catch viruses by swimming in the polluted water. Animals and plants die because of the pollution.

Child 5

V is for the vehicles.

Chemicals from power stations and factories cause air pollution. Vehicles give out poisonous gases, which contribute towards acid rain, which can harm trees and kill fish living in lakes. It can make our eyes, throat and lungs sore and can damage plants too. Lead from petrol makes pollution worse.

Child 6

E is for the earth.

The world in which we live is being spoiled. Our countryside is disappearing fast. Fields and trees are being spoiled as roads, houses and factories are being built on them. Rare flowers disappear every day. Wild animals we used to see on country walks are becoming rare. I think we need a new letter.

Child 7

Put these letters together and they make the word STARVE. What can we do now?

(The seventh child, who is standing alone, holds up the letter 'H')

Child 8

H is for help.

Let us help our world. What can we do?

Child 9

S is for the sea.

We can all help to keep the sea clean. We mustn't leave rubbish on the beach. We must take all our cans, bottles and litter home or put it in rubbish bins provided.

Child 10

T is for the trees.We can tell people about what is happening to the rainforest. We can help by planting trees and protecting those we have. We can ask our parents to think hard before buying furniture made from tropical hardwoods.

Child 11

A is for the animals.

We shouldn't encourage people who kill rare species. We shouldn't buy any coats or souvenirs that are made from animals. Fur coats, ivory and things made from crocodile skin all mean another animal has been killed just for pleasure or just so people can look good. Soon these animals may become extinct.

Child 12

R is for the rivers.

We can stop throwing rubbish in the rivers. This will make them less polluted and encourage plants and other living things to make their habitats there. We shouldn't leave any rubbish lying around. Bottles and cans found on riverbanks should be picked up and sent for recycling.

Child 13

V is for the vehicles.

We can encourage our parents to use the car less or to share with other people. We can encourage our parents to use lead free petrol. Fewer cars in our cities mean less pollution. We can walk or cycle to school instead.

Child 14

E is for the earth.

We can plant seeds in our garden. Flowers will encourage insects and birds. We can put a bird table in our garden, which will encourage the birds to come. Garden ponds will attract animals and insects too. We should follow the country code when we are in the countryside. If we all do a little bit to help the world, we will not starve. We will have a harvest for years to come

(Children rearrange the letters to make the word harvest by including the child holding the letter 'H'.)

All children

Happy Harvest everyone!

Letters available on
CD ROM refs: 05s/t/a/r/v/e/h

HARVEST 6

It is important to look at the joyous side of 'Harvest', but it is also important to consider the people of the world who are hungry and who often do not have a good harvest because of droughts and natural or man made disasters. These poems look at the happiness and sadness of harvest time.

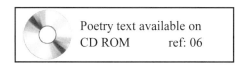

Poetry text available on
CD ROM   ref: 06

Harvest

Hurray, hurray, harvest is here,

One of the happiest times of the year.

The fruits on the tree are ready to fall,

Watch the young farmers gather
  them all.

The corn in the field is golden
  and strong

There'll be bread on the table before
  very long.

The fishermen travel far out to sea

To catch wriggling fish we have for
  our tea.

Aren't we so lucky, for we can
  celebrate,

Our harvest together on this
  special date.

No Harvest

I got up for breakfast

There wasn't any there,

That is because

The cupboard was bare.

Our land is so hot,

Our land is so dry,

When we grow our crops

They wither and die.

This year there's no harvest

Last year there was none.

The food we had stored

Is eaten and gone.

When you celebrate harvest

At this time of year,

Please say a prayer

For the people out here.

CHRISTMAS 1

Christmas is a time for giving and sharing. It is also a time of hope, when magical things can happen to make people happy. This story tells us about a family whose gifts exceeded anything they could have ever imagined.

 Illustration available on CD ROM   ref: 07

The Magic Stocking

It was Christmas Eve. Mrs Williams walked quickly down the main street. Snow was beginning to fall quite thickly.

"It's so difficult bringing up children on your own, especially at Christmas when you don't have enough money to buy presents," she thought.

Mrs Williams walked down a side street. She looked around. She'd never been down this street before. The shops were small and quaint and the windows had bubble glass in them like those of long ago. In the distance she could see the faint light from a shop window. Snow had covered most of the window. So she wiped some of it away with her hand. Inside she could see a small red stocking on display and by the side of it lay a silver bracelet. Mrs Williams turned the door handle and the bell began to ring. For a moment she stood alone in the shop. There

were lots of boxes wrapped up in Christmas paper and she noticed that they all had name tags on them. The only things left unwrapped were the small Christmas stocking and the bracelet. Everything else had obviously been bought. Just then an old lady and gentleman appeared.

"Can we help you?" asked the old lady with a smiling face.

"I'd like to buy the stocking," said Mrs Williams.

"I'm sorry, but it's not for sale," said the old man.

Mrs Williams looked at the old man. She was sure she had seen him somewhere before. He had a long white beard and red rosy cheeks. He seemed somehow familiar.

Mrs Williams looked at the bracelet. How she wished she had a bracelet like that. If she couldn't buy the stocking, then perhaps she could buy the bracelet instead. Then she remembered the children and decided that it would be very selfish. She

looked pleadingly at the old man.

"Please, please sell me the stocking," she asked.

The old man looked at Mrs Williams.

"Is it for anyone special?" he asked, "Because it is a very special stocking."

"Yes, it's for my children Benjamin and Sarah," said Mrs Williams.

The old man smiled, "Well, in that case you can have it."

"How much is it?" asked Mrs Williams.

"Take it, you can have it as a Christmas present," the old man replied.

"Thank you, thank you very much," said Mrs Williams. "Have a merry Christmas."

"And you too," said the old man, with a twinkle in his eyes.

As Mrs Williams turned to go, the back door to the shop opened slightly. She thought she saw reindeer in the yard but decided she must be dreaming and blinked. She looked again but the yard was quite empty. A reindeer in the middle of town! Whatever next?

When she got home she took the stocking out of her shopping bag. She put two oranges inside, a small bag of nuts, a bar of chocolate and some coloured crayons. She carried the stocking into the lounge and walked over to the window. The night was clear and she noticed a star that was

bigger and brighter than the rest. It shone a beam of silvery light that swirled in and out of the furniture in the room like a silvery fog. Everything it touched seemed to sparkle like diamonds. And then in the twinkling of an eye it was gone.

On Christmas morning the children rushed downstairs into the lounge where they saw the stocking.

Sarah put her hand in the stocking and pulled out a model nativity scene. She put her hand inside again and found several figures.

"Wow!" shouted Benjamin. "Mum, mum, come quickly, look what Sarah's found in the stocking."

Mrs Williams ran into the room wondering what was going on. She saw the nativity scene and the Baby Jesus in his crib. She looked surprised, as she hadn't put that inside the stocking.

"I wonder what else is in there?" asked Benjamin.

Sarah put her hand inside and pulled out a small Christmas tree followed by some fairy lights shaped like lanterns. In turn they began lifting things out of the stocking. A turkey, a Christmas cake, mince pies, decorations for the room, a computer game for Benjamin and a portable CD player for Sarah.

"That's it!" said Sarah. "There's

nothing else."

Benjamin put his hand inside the stocking.

"Look what I've found," he said.

He pulled out the tiny parcel with a name tag attached to it.

"Mum, it's for you," he said.

Mrs Williams unwrapped the parcel to reveal a small box. She lifted the lid and stared in amazement at a silver bracelet.

"Cool!" said Benjamin.

"Cor!" said Sarah.

"Well I never," said Mrs Williams. "It's the silver bracelet I saw in the shop yesterday. How on earth did it get here?"

"It must be magic," said Benjamin.

The family had a wonderful Christmas. However Mrs Williams couldn't forget the stocking. She hadn't put any of those things inside the stocking. The owners of the shop must have done it. She must go and thank them tomorrow.

The following afternoon she put on her thick woollen coat and set off into town. Eventually she found the right street. She walked up to the front of the shop and stopped suddenly. It didn't look anything like a shop. It was empty. The shelves were totally bare and there was a 'For Sale' sign nailed onto the wall. Just as she was about to turn and go, she noticed a message scrawled on the outside of the window. It said,

SANTA'S WORKSHOP
WHERE WISHES COME TRUE

Mrs Williams looked puzzled. Hadn't she wished for a happy Christmas for her children? But that was silly. Adults knew that wishes didn't come true; they only came true in fairy stories. But then… it was Christmas, and maybe wishes came true at Christmas. Perhaps if you wished hard enough and the wish was for someone you cared about, it would come true. Now she understood. Yes, she was certain, wishes could come true.

Mrs Williams took the stocking out of her pocket. She wrote a short note on a piece of paper and put it through the letter-box.

It said, "Thanks for making my wish come true."

Mrs Williams turned up the collar on her coat, it was almost dark now and the street was silent. Everywhere was white and still. Somewhere in the back of her mind she thought she could hear sleigh bells. She looked into the night sky all the way home just waiting for a glimmer… a glimmer of Santa on his sleigh!

CHRISTMAS 2

Christmas is often a time when magic appears to be in the air. Christians believe it is a time of peace and good will to all men. 'The Christmas Cactus' is the story of a flower who has been grumpy all his life and isn't liked by all the other flowers. However, on Christmas morning he turns over a new leaf and as a result becomes very beautiful.

Illustration available on CD ROM   ref: 08

The Christmas Cactus

A long time ago the world was very simple. All the animals looked alike. The birds were identical and even their beaks were the same length. The fish in the seas were the same colour and even the insects looked identical.

It was in those days that Mr and Mrs Caremore had the difficult job of looking after the world. One spring they began to hear voices of discontentment echoing through the forests and the fields.

"I'm fed up of being like you," said one flower.

"And I'm fed up of being like you," said another one.

"I want to be different," said the first flower.

"So do I," said the other one.

"Well, let's do something about it," said the first flower.

"I agree," said the other one.

The flowers set off to the hollow tree where Mr and Mrs Caremore lived. Mr and Mrs Caremore listened with interest.

"I think you're right, you should be different," said Mr Caremore.

"However, it's a difficult job. We can't just change you all in one day. We'll have to do it gradually. Come back soon and we'll be able to give you new identities."

The Caremores set to work. Mr Caremore was an excellent artist. He sat down at his easel and began to draw. How was he going to make each flower different?

"I know," he said, "they can have different shaped leaves and different coloured petals. And some can be small and some can be tall."

"And they can smell different too," said Mrs Caremore.

"What a good idea," said Mr Caremore.

Mr and Mrs Caremore worked hard all year designing new flowers. By Christmas Eve the designs were done. They called all the flowers over to their home in the hollow tree.

"There are lots of different designs for

you to choose from," they said. "Just look at all the pictures on the wall and choose the design you like best."

The flowers couldn't wait to choose. Quickly they chose the prettiest, buttercups, daisies, daffodils and roses. By nightfall all the designs had been chosen except for one.

"No one will choose this one," said Mrs Caremore, looking at the only design left on the wall.

"I know, it's not very pretty is it? But I couldn't think of any more designs," said Mr Caremore sadly.

The last design had a very thick stem. It was green and prickly and very ugly. It was a cactus.

"This design must belong to someone," said Mr Caremore. "I drew a design for each flower. There must be a flower without a new identity."

"Don't worry about it now," said Mrs Caremore, "Perhaps the owner will call tomorrow."

There was one flower that hadn't claimed his new identity. His name was Prickles. The other flowers called him Prickles because he had a prickly nature.

"Don't bother with him," they'd say. "He's very grumpy."

Some of the younger flowers teased Prickles They would run up behind him and pull his leaves or twist his stem.

"Get away," he'd say. "Leave me alone."

"Ha ha, hee hee, you're Mr Prickly," they'd shout, before running off into the woods.

The morning after the flowers had gained their new identity was Christmas morning. Mr Prickles woke up to the sound of youngsters playing in the snow. He looked once, he looked twice and was surprised to see they all looked so different, different

colours, shapes and sizes.

"What's happened to you all?" he asked.

"Mr and Mrs Caremore have given us new identities," they shouted with glee.

"But why didn't you tell me?" asked Mr Prickles.

"We didn't think you'd want a new identity, we thought you were happy being grumpy," said a beautiful blue flower with bell shaped leaves.

"But that's not true! I would love a new identity, a second chance."

"I'm sorry, but I think you're too late," said the blue flower. "Mr and Mrs Caremore are going on holiday for Christmas. They've probably set off by now."

"Perhaps I can catch them if I hurry," said Mr Prickles setting off into the wood.

There was no time to follow the path; he'd have to take the short cut. There was lots of undergrowth and bushes with thorns barred his way. They scratched his leaves and cut into his stem, but still he struggled on until he eventually came to their home. He knocked on the door loudly.

"Please let me in," he shouted. "I've come for my new identity."

There was no answer.

Suddenly the door swung open and the breeze blew him inside. He looked around the room. There was one picture left hanging on the wall. He looked at it very closely. What an ugly flower he thought, all green and prickly with no petals. Underneath the picture was a small box. Inside the box was the new design. He lifted out his new costume and put it on. He looked in the mirror and began to cry.

"It serves me right for being so grumpy," he said. "If I hadn't been so awful to the other flowers in the first place, then perhaps they would have told me about the new designs."

His head began to hurt. He rubbed it and noticed red blood. He must have caught himself on the thorns in the forest.

"I do want to turn over a new leaf," he said. "I'm not really a prickly old character."

Then he looked in the mirror again and stared in disbelief. Where the trickle of blood had been there was a bright red flower and every other cut and graze had become a bright red flower too.

"I'm not so ugly after all," he said beaming, "I'm a Christmas cactus."

CHRISTMAS 3

Christmas is a time when many people give presents to family and friends. This story makes us realise that it is not how much we spend that is important, but the thought that lies behind the giving. 'Rabbit's Present' tells us the story of a rabbit who goes in search of a present to give to the one she loves. When she comes home without a present she is sad, but just by returning home she has made someone very happy.

 Illustration available on
CD ROM   ref: 09

Rabbit's Present

Jeremy and Snowy were white rabbits. They lived in a hutch at the bottom of Janet's garden. Janet loved her white rabbits very much. Every morning she would bring them fresh dandelion leaves for their breakfast and at night when she came home from school she would play with them. She would open the hutch and let both rabbits run around the lawn until it was time for tea.

Just a week before Christmas while Janet was at school, Sam the dog and Tiny the cat came running down the garden path. Sam was barking. Tiny the cat jumped onto the top of the hutch for safety.

"I'm not getting down from here until you promise not to chase me any more," said Tiny, stretching out her claws angrily.

"I'm not chasing you," said Sam. "I'm trying to tell you something."

"What?" asked Tiny, peeping over the edge of the hutch.

"It's nearly Christmas," said Sam.

"What's Christmas?" asked Tiny.

"Don't you know anything?" said Sam shaking his head.

He told Tiny all about Christmas, about Mary and Joseph and the baby Jesus and about Father Christmas.

"I wonder if he'll bring us any presents?" asked Tiny.

"I should think so," said Sam. "He brought me some last year."

Tiny jumped off the rabbit hutch and ran off up the garden path with Sam following close behind.

Snowy pushed her nose up to the wire.

"Jeremy, I'd like to buy Janet a present for Christmas," she said.

"How on earth can you do that," he replied. "You're stuck in this cage all day and when Janet lets you out, you're not allowed to go very far."

"I'll think of something," she said and settled down for a nap.

On Christmas Eve it started to snow. At first the flakes were very small and

28

they melted when they touched the ground but then they got bigger and bigger. Soon the ground was covered in a white blanket.

The garden was still and quiet. Janet and her mother had gone Christmas shopping and the dog and cat were indoors. When Janet came home she ran down the path excitedly.

"It's nearly Christmas," she shouted. "It's nearly Christmas."

Snowy began to sneeze; once; twice; three times.

"Oh dear me," said Janet. "You've got a cold. I had better bring you inside and put you by the fire."

She opened the hutch. Just as she was about to pick Snowy up, the rabbit spied her chance and leapt out of the cage. She ran up the path as fast as she could.

"Come back!" shouted Janet, but Snowy was gone.

Snowy didn't stop running until she reached the end of the lane.

"What a good plan," thought Snowy. "I haven't really got a cold at all. This was my plan to get free. And now I'm out, I'll go and find a Christmas present for Janet to show her how much I love her.

Snowy didn't realise how unhappy she'd made Janet feel. Janet was crying and whatever her mother said or did, it didn't make Janet feel any better.

"You're going to get some lovely presents from Father Christmas tomorrow," said her mother.

"I don't want any," said Janet. "I want my rabbit."

Snowy ran up the road. It was getting dark and the lights were coming on in the shop windows.

"What I need is a shop," thought Snowy.

She saw a bright light ahead of her.

"That must be a shop," she said.

She hopped inside and looked around. This was no good. It sold paint and wallpaper. Snowy ran outside and into another shop. There were lots of people sitting at tables. They were drinking and eating.

"Would you like a pint of beer?" asked a man with a moustache.

"No thanks," said Snowy hopping out of the door and into the street.

She hopped on up the street. In the distance she could see lots of bright lights. She ran inside the shop. There were lampshades and chandeliers hanging from the ceiling.

"Hey, there's a rabbit in here!" shouted the owner. "Catch it!"

Snowy jumped up onto the table and knocked over a pretty white lamp. It fell on the floor with a crash. The owner tripped over the wire and two more lamps came crashing down.

"Watch out for the Christmas tree," said the owner.

But it was too late. Snowy ran straight into the Christmas tree. It fell over on top of her. The floor was covered with tinsel, fairy lights and coloured baubles. Snowy ran out of the shop and down the street. The owner stood at the door shaking his fist.

When Snowy got home it was late. Everyone else was in bed and the hutch was locked. She went round to the front door and squeezed through the letterbox. She could hear someone crying. She hopped upstairs and found Janet sitting up in bed crying into a white handkerchief.

"I'm home," said Snowy. "I'm sorry but I couldn't find a present for you. I'm really sorry."

She hopped onto the bed beside Janet. Janet lifted her head and squealed with delight.

"Mum, Dad, come and see what Father Christmas has brought me," she shouted.

Her parents came rushing into the room to see what all the fuss was about. They all began to laugh.

Snowy couldn't understand what they were all laughing about until Janet picked her up and took her over to the mirror. She stared into the mirror and chuckled. Yes, she did look funny. She was just like a Christmas present. She was covered in Christmas decorations from head to foot. She had tinsel on her back and round her neck and baubles dangling from both ears.

"What a wonderful present," said Janet smiling, "the best I've ever had."

CHRISTMAS 4

Christmas is a wonderful time of year for children. Many like to hear the story of Jesus' birth. The story, 'Katie goes to the stable' tells us about a small lamb who experiences the excitement of the visiting angels and how she is chosen to go to Bethlehem with the shepherds.

Illustration available on
CD ROM   ref: 10

Katie Goes to the Stable

David the shepherd boy was looking after his sheep on the hillside. His friends had gone home for tea. David knew they would return later to take over the watch. David had been keeping watch since early morning and he was tired.

"I'm going to have a nap now," he said to the sheep, "but you must promise not to wander off."

All the sheep except for one nodded their heads. The one that didn't was Katie. She was only a few weeks old and very energetic and full of life. She was mischievous and longed for excitement and adventure. She decided she would run to the top of the hill to see what was on the other side. While her mother's back was turned she bounded off up the hillside.

"Wow!" she exclaimed when she saw the surrounding countryside below her. "What a big world I live in. And look at that town down there. That must be Bethlehem. I'd love to visit and say hello to the people there. Perhaps I could find a friend to play with. That would be fun."

She lay down on the ground and looked around.

"I've got a funny feeling in my bones that something special is going to happen tonight," she said with expectation.

She looked up into the night sky. The sky was clear and the stars twinkled down at her. One of them was bigger and brighter than the rest.

"That's strange!" she thought. "I've never seen a bright star like that before. I'll go and tell the others."

Katie ran down the hill to where David was sleeping. She could see his friends running up the hill to where the flock was grazing. They were pointing at the star that Katie had seen and were shouting for David to wake up.

"Wake up, Wake up!" Katie bleated, nuzzling David's warm neck, "Something is happening."

David jumped up quickly. "What's the matter?" he asked wearily.

But before Katie could answer, a bright light appeared in the sky and an angel appeared before them.

"Don't be afraid," said the angel, "I've brought you some good news. A baby has been born in Bethlehem. He is your Saviour, Christ the Lord. Follow the star to Bethlehem and you will find the baby Jesus in a stable."

David was frightened and stood there mesmerised. The other boys stood behind him wondering what was happening. They watched while a

31

present for a baby king.

"We'll take Katie, I'm sure the baby would like a lamb," said David excitedly.

The shepherds followed the bright star to Bethlehem. They came to the stable. Quietly, they opened the door and saw Jesus lying on a bed of straw.

David carried Katie to where Mary and Joseph were watching over the baby Jesus.

"I have brought the baby a present," said David.

Joseph looked at the lamb. "What a lovely present," he said, "I am sure that Jesus will like her."

The shepherds stayed a while and watched the baby Jesus sleeping. Katie fell asleep on the hay, happy to have found a new friend. But soon it was time for the shepherds to leave. They said their goodbyes.

"Look after the little boy," said David to the lamb. "He is going to be a special man one day."

"I know," said Katie. "I knew it, right from the moment I climbed to the top of the hill and saw the star. For this is the first Christmas, and for many years to come, Christains will remember this day and give thanks to the Lord for sending this baby boy."

crowd of angels appeared before them praising God. Then just as quickly as they had appeared, the angels disappeared.

"We must go and see the baby," said David.

"We must take him a present," said another.

"But what can we give him?" another one asked.

Katie bounded over saying, "Take me, take me. I would so like to see the baby."

David looked down at the lamb. She was so pure and white, just the right

CHRISTMAS 5

Sometimes people forget the real meaning of Christmas. In this day and age, we are surrounded by commercialism. Shops and advertising encourage us to think that Christmas is about buying and receiving presents. Christians believe children should be reminded about the real meaning of Christmas. We should think about giving, sharing and being thankful for our families and home comforts. We should also think about all the people who will not have the essentials for survival. The poem, 'Letters to Santa', looks at two children from different lands. One child has everything, but wants and expects more; the other child has nothing and wants only a chance to live.

 Poetry text available on
CD ROM   ref: 11

Letter to Santa - 1

My Christmas Shopping List
Dear Father Christmas
I am writing to you
A list of all the things I want
And a list of things you can do.
My bicycle is rusty, so
Could you send me a mountain bike?
A helmet and a saddlebag
Are things that I would like.
I know I've got a computer
But it's really out of date,
So could I have a PC
If it's not too late.
The snooker table I got last year
Is really far too small
So could I have a bigger one?
A cue and set of balls.
Could I have a CD player?
And a camera with a zoom
And what about a T.V?
I need one in my room.
And could I have a puppy?
My parrot's not much fun
And my Persian cat ignores me
He just lies there in the sun.
And by the way, the usual
Chocolates, sweets and candy,
Bubble bath and felt tip pens
They always come in handy.
I'll be signing off now
I've lots of things to do
Don't forget my presents
And make sure they'll all brand new.

Letter to Santa - 2

Dear Father Christmas,
I am writing this to you
In hope that you will hear my prayer
For there's something you can do.
I do not need a turkey
Or fairy on the tree
And trimmings from the ceiling
Are pointless here you see.
Please don't send me crackers
Or stockings filled with sweets,
Peanuts, crisps and sausage rolls
To me are all rare treats.
I do not need a video
Or a doll that can wet
I cannot read so don't send books
Nor do I need a cricket set.

Please don't send a skate board
And a set of felt tip pens
Or a pair of new binoculars
With telescopic lens.
Look down at my family
For shelter we have none
Our clothes are all in tatters
Our food supplies have gone.
Disease is spreading wildly
Our people falling ill
No doctors here or nurses
No medicine or pills.
Take pity on us this Christmas
And take away a tear
For life's worth more than presents
In this wilderness out here.

CHRISTMAS 6

Children often like to hear stories about our Christmas customs. The story, 'The Christmas Fairy', tells a magical story about how we come to have a fairy at the top of the tree.

 Illustration available on CD ROM   ref: 12

The Christmas Fairy

It was Christmas Eve and the snow was falling gently down on the roofs and gardens. Susie was sitting on the rug by the fire. She was gazing up at the Christmas tree that she had helped to decorate earlier in the week.

"What I can't understand," said Susie, "is why we have a fairy at the top of the tree. It's a funny place for a fairy to be, isn't it Mum?"

"Well, no, not really. Have I not told you why we have a fairy at the top of the tree?" asked Mum.

"No," answered Susie.

"Well, I'll tell you now. Come and sit on my knee," said her Mum.

Susie climbed onto her mother's knee and made herself comfortable.

"A long time ago there lived a band of fairies. They were good fairies and they only did kind things. When the fairies grew up they would go to the fairy queen's house in the roots of an old oak tree. She would give them a special job to do. Well, it was Christmas Eve and all the newly grown up fairies had gone to the queen's house. One by one they went inside to see what job they had to do. Pearl, a happy, smiling fairy went in first."

"Hello Pearl," said the fairy queen, "there's a job I'd like you especially to do. When children lose one of their teeth, they put it under their pillow. I'd like you to fly over to each child's house, take the tooth away and in its place put a silver coin. You will be called the Tooth Fairy."

"Thank you," said Pearl, "I can't wait to start."

Pearl flew off delightedly, her white teeth glistening brightly.

To Willow, she gave the job of painting the leaves in the autumn.

"Take this paint box and when the weather gets cooler, you must fly around the wood and paint every single leaf," said the fairy queen.

"Thank you," said Willow flying away with the paint box firmly tucked under her arm.

To Silky, she gave the job of insect polisher.

"I would like you to polish all the beetles' backs until they are bright and shiny. Now take this tin of black polish and go on your way," said the fairy queen.

Silky flew off happily clutching the tin of polish in her hand.

To Rose Water she gave the job of sewing on rose petals.

"You are an excellent seamstress and so I give you the job of sewing on rose petals," said the fairy queen.

Rose Water flew away quite happily with a needle and a selection of coloured threads. Then the fairy queen looked out of her window.

"Well that looks like it for this year. I think it's time I went on my yearly Christmas visit to the world of children," she said.

She locked her front door and flew off into the starry night sky.

A few minutes later, one little fairy arrived at the front door. She was late because she had been skating with some younger fairies on the frozen fishpond.

"Hello, is anybody there?" shouted the fairy through the keyhole.

There was no answer. Then the little fairy heard a voice, a small brown bird appeared on the lowest branch.

"I'm afraid you're too late Silver, the fairy queen has gone away," said the small brown wren.

"Oh no!" sighed Silver looking rather upset, "I came for a job. What am I going to do now? All the other fairies have gone. What am I going to do this Christmas?"

"I don't know. You'll not get a job now, you're too late. It's Christmas Day tomorrow," said the wren cheekily as he flew away.

"I will get a job," said Silver stubbornly, "just you wait and see."

But it was already getting dark. The snow was falling thickly and the forest was filled with eerie sounds. Silver sat down on the roots of the old tree and cried. Her silver tears fell on her dress like star drops. She was alone for Christmas. Then out of the blue, a sudden breeze sprang up and a small twig fell from the branch above her and landed at her feet. She picked up the twig and began to wave it in the air.

"I know what I'll do," she thought, "I'll fly through the sky this Christmas waving this branch and I'll pretend it can do magic. Perhaps I can make it do magic for me and then I can get a job."

And as if by magic, a small snowflake landed on the end of the wand and it began to sparkle in the darkness.

"I've got a magic wand," she shouted excitedly. "A magic wand! I'm a real fairy now!"

Waving the wand in the cold air, Silver flew off into the darkness. Moments later she came to a village. She could see a cottage in the distance and there was a light shining through one of the windows. Silver peered inside.

"Oh doesn't this look lovely. Look at the decorations and the presents under the tree. Perhaps I can spend my Christmas here and maybe they would find a job for me too," she said shivering.

"But how I wish I was inside by the fire," she thought.

She pointed her wand at the window. And suddenly there she was by the dying fire. It really was a magic wand. Everyone was in bed. The room was quiet and still. Then Silver noticed the Christmas tree lights shining brightly in the corner of the room. It was only then that Silver realised she had lost her homemade wand.

"Oh no," she cried, "I've lost my magic wand; I'll never get a job now!"

Then she had a brilliant idea "Perhaps if I climb to the top of the tree I might be able to see where I dropped it," she thought.

Silver began climbing the tree. At first it did not seem so very far to the top, but with every step she took it seemed another step away. Eventually she reached the top of the tree and gave a loud yawn. She looked around the room but she couldn't see the wand anywhere.

"I feel so tired," thought Silver, "It's far too late to look for my wand now. I think I'll take a nap and look for it tomorrow."

She made herself comfortable among the branches and soon fell asleep.

The next morning she was woken by the sounds of delighted children. She jumped up and straightened her silvery, white dress and shook the creases out of her wings. She could hear the children talking excitedly.

"Look at the fairy at the top of the tree," said the little girl, "Isn't she beautiful."

"Mummy must have put her there in the night," said the little boy.

"I didn't put her there," said Mummy, "I think she appeared by magic. It's the first time I've ever seen a fairy at the top of a tree. She looks so lovely, I think we'll have one again next year."

"What a good idea," said the little girl.

Silver looked down at the children and smiled. "I've done it," she thought. "I've found myself a job. I can be the fairy at the top of the tree every year."

"And from that day on, people have been putting fairies at the top of their Christmas trees," said Mum.

"That was a lovely story," said the little girl looking up at the fairy at the top of the tree.

And as she closed her eyes and began thinking of Christmas day, she thought she heard a little voice say, "I told you I would get a job didn't I!"

CHRISTMAS 7

The poem, 'Who is It?' tells us about the excitement children experience waiting for Santa to arrive during the night of Christmas Eve.

 Poetry text available on CD ROM   ref: 13

Who is it?

Who is it?
Who has a beard of white,
And a coat of red,
Who visits all the houses,
When the children are in bed?
Santa!

Who is it?
Who comes while you're asleep,
On Christmas Eve night,
And lands on the rooftop,
When the stars are shining bright?
Santa!

Who is it?
Who comes down the chimney,
Carrying on his back,
Presents for the children,
In a great big sack?
Santa!

Who is it?
Who enjoys a tasty meal,
A sherry or a glass of wine,
A fresh mince pie,
At Christmas time?
Santa!

Who is it?
Who fills your stockings,
With presents galore,
And leaves snowy footprints,
On the bedroom floor?
Santa!

NEW YEAR 1

This story takes place in a small mining town in the 1960s. It is about a boy who is permanently dirty until one New Year's Eve when something happens to change his ways. It teaches the boy self respect and gives him self-esteem.

Illusration available on
CD ROM   ref: 14

The New Year's Resolution

Sam was eleven years old. He lived with his mum, dad and younger sister in a terraced house in the centre of the town.

Sam was one of those boys who always looked dirty. He would set off for school looking smart and clean but by the time he returned, he was a real mess. He'd have mud all over his shoes from playing football on the wet field, grass stains and dirty marks all over his pants from having play fights, his shirt would be hanging out and his hair would look like it had never been combed. And although he'd be covered in muck from head to toe he'd have to be forced to have a shower. He wasn't only untidy in his appearance; his schoolwork was just as bad. The teachers expected Sam to hand in messy work and so Sam never bothered to try any harder.

"I'm just a mess," he'd joke to his friends, as though he didn't care. But inside Sam was sad. He wanted to be clean and neat, like his sister, but he found it so difficult that he gave up trying.

"I like being dirty," he'd say to himself in the mirror. But even he didn't like what he saw. His hair was ruffled. His face was dirty. He had stains on his jumper. His fingernails were long and jagged and dirty. "It's more fun being dirty," he'd say, trying to smile.

Sam's mum didn't know what to do with him.

"Don't you care about yourself?" she'd ask.

Sam shrugged his shoulders.

"I like myself the way I am," he'd say with a big grin.

"You ought to be ashamed of yourself," said his father.

Sam was ashamed of himself but he just smiled and laughed it off.

That New Year's Eve something happened to Sam that changed his life. It was lunchtime and all the family were sitting around the table. Mum began talking about New Year's resolutions.

"What is a New Year's resolution?" asked Carole, Sam's younger sister.

"It's a promise you make; something you'll do for the whole year," replied Mum. "I'm going to go on a diet."

"I'll stop smoking," said Dad

"I'll keep my bedroom tidy," said Carole.

Sam said nothing.

"What about you Sam?" asked Mum.

"I can't think of one," said Sam.

"Well, I've got a good one for you," said Mum. "How about having a shower every night?"

"Ugh, I'm not doing that," said Sam. "Dad, I bet you never made any New Year's resolutions like that when you were my age."

"Well, no I didn't, but I did go first footing," he replied.

"What's that?" asked Sam.

"When I was a boy I lived in Scotland, and we used to have a party on New Year's Eve. I was always allowed to go first footing. I'd go out the back door, get a piece of coal from the coalbunker and come in through the front door when the clock struck twelve. Then I'd wish everyone a happy new year. The piece of coal was supposed to bring good luck."

Sam asked if he could go first footing at the New Year's party.

"You're too young to be staying up so late," said Mum.

"Please Mum, can I? All the family

Sam ran across the yard towards the coalbunker. It was dark and very icy. Suddenly he slipped and fell head first into the coalbunker.

"Ouch!" he shouted, climbing out of the coalbunker with a piece of coal in his hand.

He heard the clock strike twelve and ran as fast as he could down the street to the front door. He knocked three times. The lights in the hall came on and the door was opened wide. He could see lots of smiling faces.

"Happy New Year," he shouted.

Then there were screams of laughter.

"Who is it?" asked one voice.

"I think it's a chimney sweep," said another.

Some of the guests were crying with laughter.

"What's so funny?" asked Sam.

"Have a look in the mirror," said his sister giggling.

Sam ran upstairs to the bathroom and looked in the mirror. His face and hands were totally black; even his clothes. He hadn't realised that when he had fallen into the coalbunker he had got covered in coal dust. He looked terrible.

Without thinking, he took his dirty clothes off and jumped in the shower. That felt better. Then he put on some clean clothes, combed his hair and

will be here and there's no school," pleaded Sam.

"Okay, I suppose so," said Mum, "but any trouble and you're off to bed."

Sam smiled.

Family and friends came to the New Year party and it was great fun. Everyone looked smart…. except Sam. He had his scruffy old jeans on and, of course, he hadn't washed.

It was five minutes to twelve. Everyone was getting excited. Sam was sent out the back door to get a piece of coal.

"Don't knock on the door until you hear the clock strike twelve," said Mum.

went downstairs. Everyone stopped what they were doing and stared.

"Just look at Sam. Well I never," said Auntie Jean.

"He's setting an example isn't he? The first one to begin a New Year resolution," said Uncle Bob.

"I don't believe it," said Mum. "You had a shower!"

Sam couldn't understand what all the fuss was about. He looked in the lounge mirror, and then looked again. He couldn't believe his eyes. Was that really him in the mirror? Sam saw a smart young man in a clean white shirt and pressed trousers, a young man with shiny hair and a clean face and hands. No it couldn't be. He looked again. Yes, a smart young man was he.

"Well," said Sam, "I'm starting this year as I mean to go on. My New Year's resolution is to be clean and smart. I'm going to keep my promise…. Well, I'll do my best."

And from that day on Sam was the cleanest, smartest boy in the whole town. Well, most of the time anyway.

NEW YEAR 2

Some people go through life thinking they are very ordinary. They don't realise what their strengths are and what special abilities they have. 'What Did You Learn Last Year?' tells the story of a boy who doesn't realise all that he has achieved, until his teacher helps him.

Illustration available on CD ROM   ref: 15

What did you learn last year?

It was the first day back at school after the Christmas holidays. The children in Mrs Jones' class were very excited. They couldn't wait to tell their friends about all the presents they'd received and the exciting things they had done. After assembly, Mrs Jones gave all the children a piece of paper.

"I want you to write down all the things you achieved last year," she said. "Make a long list."

"Please Mrs Jones, I don't understand what you mean?" said Paul.

Mrs Jones looked at Paul. "I want you to tell me all the things that you learned last year."

"Oh," said Paul, looking puzzled.

The children picked up their pencils and set to work. Paul looked at his blank piece of paper. What did he do last year? He couldn't remember. He didn't do anything. He looked around at the other children. They were all busy writing.

Paul nudged the boy next to him and whispered, "What did you learn?"

"Ssh," said the boy, "you're supposed

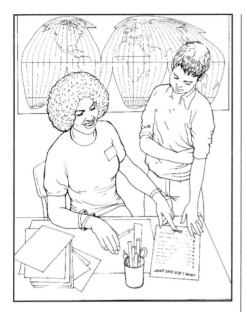

"Oh, you are silly," she said, "of course you did something last year, everybody did. Come to my desk, bring your pencil and paper and we'll have a think."

Paul wiped away his tears and went over to the teacher's desk. He liked Mrs Jones, she was really kind.

"I really didn't do anything last year," he said, beginning to cry again.

"Of course you did," said Mrs Jones. "Let's think about all the things you did out of school first."

Paul looked glum, "I can't think of anything."

to be working."

Paul looked around the classroom for ideas and shook his head. He couldn't think of anything. Soon the bell sounded for playtime. Mrs Jones stood up from behind her desk. "Right children, if you've finished, you can go out to play."

All the children stood up and went to get their coats. Paul stayed on his chair. He looked at his empty paper.

"What's the matter Paul?" asked Mrs Jones.

"I didn't do anything last year," he said.

"Oh dear," said Mrs Jones, "let me have a look at your paper."

She walked over to his table and looked at the blank piece of paper.

"Well," said Mrs Jones, "I remember your mum telling me that you swam a length at the swimming baths. She also said you started playing football at the Leisure Centre."

"Oh yes, I forgot about those things," said Paul, beginning to smile and writing them down on his piece of paper.

"And what did you do at school?" asked Mrs Jones.

"I can't remember," said Paul.

"Dear me," said Mrs Jones. "You did lots of things. You learned how to do joined up writing and you climbed to the top of the ropes in the school hall for the first time."

"Oh yes, I remember now," said Paul writing them down.

"And don't you remember last summer you came first in the running race on Sports Day? You won an award for good behaviour too."

"I forgot about those things," said Paul writing them down as fast as he could.

"And don't forget Christmas," said Mrs Jones.

"Why, what did I do then?"

"You won first prize in the fancy dress competition."

"Oh yes," said Paul, that wasn't so long ago."

"Now let's have a look at your piece of paper."

"Cor," said Paul looking down at the paper in front of him. "I've filled it up."

"What did I tell you," said Mrs Jones, smiling.

"Did I do all those things last year?" he asked.

"You certainly did," said Mrs Jones. "Didn't you do well? Now put your coat on and go out to play, you've got to do just as much this year."

"I certainly will," said Paul. "I certainly will."

NEW YEAR 3

'December' tells the story of a fairy who is very sad because the year is nearly over. This story suggests we should never be sad when the year is over. Instead, we should be happy because there are so many things to look forward to.

 Illustration available on CD ROM   ref: 16

December

December the woodland fairy was very sad. She sat on a toadstool under the tallest pine tree in the forest and cried. The tears trickled down her rosy cheeks and onto her crimson dress. Wise Owl heard her cries. He landed on a branch above her head.

"What's the matter?" he asked.

"It's New Year's Eve," she muttered.

"But why are you crying? It's a happy time."

"Oh no it isn't," she spluttered.

"Why ever not?" he asked, becoming concerned.

"Well, the month is nearly over. You only employed me for December. A new fairy will take my place next month. Whatever will happen to me? You'll have no use for me."

"Oh, you are silly," he said, flying down beside her.

He put one of his wings around her shoulders to shelter her from the wind and snow.

"Of course, you're a new fairy. You've never done this kind of work before. I should have told you when you applied for the job."

"What should you have told me?" said December, wiping her tears with a white petal handkerchief.

"I should have told you that this job wasn't just for one month only. We're going to need you again this time next year."

"Next year?" she replied.

"Of course," he said. "We'll need you to help decorate the Christmas tree and bring presents to the children. We'll need you to tell the children all about the baby Jesus born in Bethlehem, and most of all, we'll need you to be the fairy at the top of the Christmas tree."

December put away her handkerchief and smiled.

Wise owl looked at her and said, "Now, you've worked very hard this month, so, take the rest of the year off. Have a good holiday and we'll see you again on December the first."

"Really?" she shouted, jumping off the toadstool and dancing with glee.

"Yes, of course, we're going to need you every year," he said, ruffling his feathers. "Anyway, I can't stay any longer, got to dash, January's waiting for me."

"January?"

"Yes, she's my new fairy for next month. She'll start her job as soon as the clock strikes midnight."

Wise Owl spread his wings and took off into the frosty night air.

"Goodbye December," he said, disappearing into the frosty night sky. "See you again next year."

LENT LEADING UP TO EASTER
Shrove Tuesday and Ash Wednesday

Lent is the season of the church's year when Christians prepare themselves for Easter. During Lent Christians think about the forty days when Jesus went into the wilderness to fast and prepare himself for his life of preaching and teaching.

Shrove Tuesday is a Christian festival and the name given to the day before Lent begins. Shrove comes from the word, 'shriven', which means to confess. Long ago people went to church to say sorry for all the things they had done wrong and the priest offered God's forgiveness. The cooks used up all of the food that would be given up during the period of Lent. Ingredients such as milk, eggs, flour and fat would be made into a meal of pancakes.

Due to the development of pancakes, children sometimes call Shrove Tuesday, Pancake Day. Nowadays, Shrove Tuesday is seen as a day of fun before the fasting of Lent begins.

The day after Shrove Tuesday is Ash Wednesday. Ash Wednesday is the first day of Lent. Some Christians go to church on this day and are anointed with a cross of ashes on their forehead. The Ashes are usually made from the palm leaves used during the previous year's Palm Sunday celebration. Nowadays, during the forty days of Lent, when Christians remember Jesus fasting in the desert, they too may choose to fast, by giving up something they enjoy eating such as chocolate or sweets.

EASTER – 1

Easter is an ancient spring festival. The word Easter comes from the word Eostre, the ancient Saxon goddess of spring. Eostre means 'The Dawn', and her festival celebrates the birth of new life in spring after winter. 'Wake up Spring', is a poem which celebrates the coming of spring and all the joys and excitement associated with the season.

Poetry text available on CD ROM   ref: 17

Wake Up Spring

Wake up spring

And take winter away,

For the ground has been frozen

Many a day.

The bulbs they are waiting
And ready to grow,
Tender shoots are appearing
From under the snow.

The sheep they are calling
And lying in wait,
For the farmer to arrive
With food at the gate.

The birds they are singing
In their beaks carry sticks,
For building their nests
In which to have chicks.

The pensioners they are peeping
Watching rain gently fall,
From behind crisp net curtains
They hope someone will call.

So wake up spring
And take winter away,
For life must go on
In its funny old way

EASTER 2

Easter is the most important time of the year for Christians, because they celebrate Jesus rising from the dead. The poem, 'Easter Time', tells the story of Easter beginning with Palm Sunday when Jesus rode into Jerusalem, going on to the Last Supper, the betrayal, the Crucifixion and finally the Resurrection.

 Poetry text available on
CD ROM   ref: 18

Easter Time

We share the Bread
And drink the wine,
We think of Jesus
At Easter time.

Palm Sunday
Jesus' ride,
Into Jerusalem
Friends by his side.

The Last Supper
The bread and wine,
The washing of feet
Their last suppertime.

Gethsemane
Where Jesus prayed,
Taken by the soldiers
When he was betrayed.

The unfair trial
Sentenced to die,
Hung on a cross
In a dark leaden sky.

Easter Sunday
And Christians praise,
Jesus their Saviour
Who rose from the grave.

EASTER 3

At Easter time, as for so many of the other religious festivals, certain activities distract us from the real message of the festival. On Easter Sunday, children often are given or even go hunting for eggs. In all the fun many children will not realise that the egg is often used as a symbol of new life. This story tries to explain the real meaning of Easter.

Illustration available on
CD ROM   ref: 19

The Easter Egg Hunt

It was the last day of the Spring Term. The children were excited, as there was to be an Easter egg hunt in the school grounds on Easter Sunday. Tomo, a new boy, who had recently come from Africa didn't understand what all the fuss was about.

"What is this hunt you are talking about?" he asked.

"It's quite simple," said Ivor, one of the boys in the top class. "Christians believe on Easter Sunday Jesus rose from the dead. To symbolise new life, the teachers hide eggs in the school grounds because out of eggs, comes new life. If you are lucky enough, you find some of the eggs and then you can eat them.

"Oh I see," said Tomo rather surprised, thinking what a strange custom it was. "Can I come?"

"Of course you can," said Ivor, "I'll meet you outside church on Sunday at 10 o'clock."

Easter Sunday was bright and cheerful. The sun was shining and the daffodils lined the verge outside the church like a golden crown. At 12 o'clock the bells rang and the congregation bustled their way out of church; most of them making their way to the schoolyard. Mr Bamber, the head teacher, had been busy all morning finding suitable places to hide the chocolate eggs. The

47

children lined up in the yard expectantly and with eager faces. Tomo lined up next to Ivor.

"Good luck!" shouted Ivor, "I hope you find some eggs."

"And you too," replied Tomo.

"On your marks, get set, GO!" shouted the head teacher.

The children dispersed across the grounds. Every few minutes, you could hear cries of delight as a child found one of the chocolate eggs.

"I've found one," shouted Ivor.

"Here's another," said John.

Just half an hour later the cries of delight became less frequent. It seemed as though all the eggs had been found.

"Did you find an egg, Tomo?" asked Ivor.

"No," said Tomo sadly, "I searched high and low but couldn't find any at all."

"Never mind," said Ivor. "It's your first try, maybe you'll be lucky next year."

"I suppose so," said Tomo trying not to look too upset.

One by one, the children disappeared off home. The playground looked deserted. Tomo was sitting on the front step of the school..

"I'll just take another look before I go home," he said. "There might be just a chance that one of the eggs hasn't been found."

Tomo walked to the far side of the field. A ditch separated the school from the farmer's field. Tomo walked along the edge of the ditch, balancing on the edge of the ditch and not really looking where he was going. Suddenly, he stumbled over a small branch and fell headlong into a patch of nettles. He was just about to say, "Ouch!" when he saw something in front of him. Moving the grass apart, he gazed in amazement.

"An egg, I've found an egg!"

But right before his very eyes the egg began to move. Small hairline cracks began to appear, until suddenly, a little head pushed its way out.

"This is a strange chocolate egg," said Tomo excitedly. "There's a real live chick inside."

By now the chick had pecked its way out completely and was ruffling its feathers.

"I suppose you want your mother," said Tomo.

He looked to his left and only a few strides away, was a large fat hen.

"Don't worry little chick, your mother's here," said Tomo kindly.

In just a few seconds, the chick had followed its mother back to the nest where four other newly hatched chicks were waiting.

"Well how about that," thought Tomo.

He ran across the field towards the farm gate. A group of boys were sitting on the top of the gate. He could hear them laughing. The boys were older than he and they were all talking about how many eggs they had found that morning.

"I found three," said Rob Garnett.

"I got two," said Chris Wilson

Then from behind the gate they heard Tomo's distinctive voice.

"I found one!" shouted Tomo proudly.

"One, is that all?" said Billy Murphy, a rather plump boy who was holding tightly to his three large eggs.

"Why are you so pleased?" asked Chris.

"Because it's the best egg you could ever find," replied Tomo.

"Why was it so special?" asked Billy Murphy, thinking it must have been the size of a football and covered in chocolate!

"Because it was a real live egg – and it hatched. I watched a chick being born," said Tomo.

"Cor!" chorused all the boys.

"Can we come and see it?" asked Ivor.

"Yes okay, follow me," replied Tomo.

The boys climbed over the gate into the farmer's field. They all crouched down to look at the family of chicks. The boys were as quiet as they possibly could be so as not to disturb the chicks.

"Aren't they beautiful?" whispered Ivor

"They're gorgeous," said Billy quietly. "It sure beats chocolate eggs."

All the boys nodded in agreement.

That evening Tomo went to bed early. His mother came upstairs to tuck him in.

"Did you enjoy your first Easter day in England?" his mother asked.

"Your father said that you didn't find any chocolate eggs."

"No," said Tomo, but with a smile on his face. "I found something far better than a chocolate egg. I was lucky enough to witness a new life being born, and that to me means so much more than finding all the chocolate eggs in the world. After all, that's what Easter's all about to Christians, isn't it?"

"You're so right," said his mother kissing him lightly on the cheek. "Good night son, sweet dreams."

"Good night Mum," Tomo replied.

EASTER 4

The poem, 'The Easter Bonnet', looks at the lighter, joyous side of Easter. It tells the humorous story of a lady whose Easter bonnet is decorated with six new born chicks.

 Poetry text available on CD ROM   ref: 20

Easter Bonnet

It was an Easter Sunday

When the Easter parade began,

We'd all assembled in Battersea Park

And were listening to the band.

The sun was shining brightly

Upon our London town,

People in their Sunday best

Smiling faces all around.

We'd come to see the bonnets

The ladies like to wear,

And as they came up closer

We all just stood and stared.

For this was no ordinary hat parade

For at the head of the line was my mother.

"That's a real chick she's wearing!"

Said my dad with a smile to my brother.

It really was a belter;

No ordinary hat,

For hopping around on top of her head

Was a chick, now fancy that!

And right before our very eyes

Another chick lifted its head.

"They're hatching out all over the place!"

I shouted to my uncle Ned.

In only a matter of minutes

The eggs on her head had all hatched.

My sister said, "How does she do it,

It's truly a marvellous batch?"

We watched in delight as my mother

Continued to lead the line

While six healthy chicks in unison

50

Followed her closely behind.

At the top of the path the chicks halted

The judge took a look at each one,

Then stopping in front of my mother

Said, "Where did you get those chicks from?"

My mother picked all the chicks up

And settled each one on her head

"Well it certainly is quite 'egg' squisite,

So unusual," the judge calmly said,

Backwards and forwards he wandered

Then he viewed all the hats up and down,

And then giving the cup to my mother said

"For the most 'egg' straordinary hat in this town!"

WONDERFUL WORLD 1

Children often enjoy observing seasonal changes. They look forward to each one for different reasons. However, what would it be like if there was only one season, and that season was winter?

Poetry text available on
CD ROM   ref: 21

In a World of Winter

In a World of Winter

Snow lies like a newly washed blanket, pure and white,

Snowflakes fall like soft cotton balls,

Icicles hang like daggers from frozen branches,

Children wear bobble hats and thick woollen mittens.

They scratch patterns on frozen windows and build snowmen,

They ski to school and sledge down hill sides,

They skate across lakes and throw snowballs.

In a World of Winter

Spring never comes,

The sun never shines and the air is ghostly still,

Flowers do not raise their pretty heads,

Newborn lambs don't skip and jump,

Summer never comes,

There are no holidays to the beach,

No sand castles or picnics,

There's no sun on freckled cheeks,

No clear blue skies or fluffy white clouds,

Butterflies don't dance and birds don't sing.

51

Autumn never comes,

Children don't kick leaves along woody lanes,

Squirrels don't search for nuts,

Birds don't fly away to warmer countries,

Animals don't hide away in warm holes and hollow trees,

For this is a World of Winter.

WONDERFUL WORLD 2

'The Bank Holiday' tells us about a boy who is disappointed when his family can't afford to take him to the seaside, but then enjoys himself even more on a day out to the countryside.

Illustration available on CD ROM   ref: 22

The Bank Holiday

It was the Bank Holiday weekend. Three days away from school. I couldn't wait to get home. Sally, my younger sister trailed behind me, skipping and singing her favourite song. I couldn't wait for Monday. Mum and Dad always took us to Blackpool for the day. We'd go on the beach first and have a ride on the donkeys. If it was warm enough we would take our shoes and socks off and paddle in the sea. Afterwards we'd go on the tram along the promenade

to the Pleasure Beach. We'd go on all the rides and eat hot dogs with ketchup oozing out of them. Then we'd walk along the pier. Dad would give us money for the slot machines. We'd lose it all in minutes. On the way home we'd stop at the fish and chip shop and eat chips out of the paper. It would be brilliant.

Sally and I walked into the kitchen. Mum was making the tea. Dad was at the table reading the paper. He spent a lot of time at home now that he was out of work. He used to work at the crisp factory but they shut down three months ago. Dad never smiled anymore. He just sat around drinking tea and smoking. Sometimes when I was in bed at night, I'd hear him and mum arguing about the price of food and school clothes.

I tapped Dad on the shoulder.

"How about a game of football Dad?" I asked.

"Not now son, perhaps at the weekend, or on Monday," he replied.

"But we can't play on Monday, we're going to Blackpool aren't we?"

"I'm sorry son, we won't be going this year."

"But why not? We always go!" I shouted.

Dad got up and went into the lounge.

"Mum? Why can't we go to Blackpool?" I asked.

"Look Mike, we're short of money. Perhaps we could do something else," she said.

"I don't want to do anything else!" I shouted. "It's not fair!"

I ran upstairs and slammed the bedroom door.

On Saturday it rained all day. Tim rang to see if I wanted to go over to his house to play on his computer. I said I didn't feel like it. I stayed in my bedroom sulking and reading the Beano. I wrote a DO NOT DISTURB sign and put it on the door.

On Sunday morning Danny called to see if I was going to Church Parade. He was in our cub pack. I told Mum to tell him I had a really bad headache.

On Monday morning the alarm went off at 8 o'clock. I'd just turned it off and rolled over to go back to sleep when Sally came rushing into the room.

"We're going on a picnic," she shouted. "We're going on a picnic!"

"So what!" I said, burying my face under the covers. If we weren't going to Blackpool I wasn't going anywhere.

"Come on Mike, get up," she said shaking my arm.

"No!" I shouted, "Go away!"

Sally went away disappointedly. I lay in bed feeling grumpy and fed up, but I had made up my mind. I was staying right here under the covers and under no circumstances was I moving!

Then I heard Sally singing in the bathroom and Mum clattering the pots and pans in the kitchen. There was a delicious smell of sausage rolls too. I could here Dad whistling as he carried the ladder up the stairs to the loft. He was going to fetch the picnic stove. I tried to ignore everything that was going on.

Then Dad shouted, "Mike, come and help me get the picnic stove out of the loft."

I didn't reply, but lay still in the darkness, pretending I wasn't there. Minutes later there was calm.

53

"Mike, are you coming?" called Mum, from the bottom of the stairs

I hesitated… then quickly grabbed my clothes and ran down stairs half dressed.

We set off in the car. Mum had chosen the destination. It was called Yellow Hills. Mum and Dad used to go there before they were married.

We parked in a lay-by and climbed over a stile into the field. Mum put the blanket on the ground and Dad opened the picnic stove. This was the Yellow Hills! Not exactly what I had expected. One hill – not yellow but very green, a small wood and a tiny stream!

Mum put the food on a clean white cloth. It was mouth watering. There were egg sandwiches, ham sandwiches, pork pies, crisps and sausage rolls. There were iced buns, an apple pie and sarsparilla to drink. It was brilliant.

After we'd eaten, Sally picked up her tennis racket.

"Let's play rounders," she said.

"But we need a rounders bat," I said, "and anyway you don't know how to play."

I was surprised… Sally could play! She hit the ball really hard. Dad jumped to catch it but it flew straight over his head and landed with a splash in the stream. I took off my socks and shoes and fished it out. Then we made a dam and collected tiddlers in a jam jar.

Afterwards we went for a walk in the woods. Sally wanted to play hide and seek. She counted to one hundred while we all ran away. I hid under a bush among the damp leaves and branches. Sally ran off in the opposite direction. She found Mum behind a tree and Dad hiding behind a fallen log. Then they all came to find me. I lay still and watched, my heart beating faster as they got closer and closer. When they had gone I crawled on my belly to a dry spot and waited. They called and called, they searched and searched, but they still couldn't find me.

"Here I am!" I shouted, jumping from my hide out and brushing the leaves from my clothes.

"We thought we'd lost you," said Mum with a worried look on her face.

"He's a big lad now," said Dad, ruffling my hair.

"And now for a race," he said. "First one back to the car gets the last sausage roll!"

He put Sally on his shoulders and we raced through the wood shouting at the top of our voices. On Tuesday I met Tim on the way to school.

"How was your trip to Blackpool?" I asked.

"What a day!" he replied. "Barry got car sick. Dad cut his foot on some glass while we were playing football. I lost my five-pound note. And on the way back we got stuck in a traffic jam and it took us three hours to get home! What about you?"

"We went on a picnic," I said smiling, "It was brilliant!"

WONDERFUL WORLD 3

The story, 'Sunshine Beach', tells us how a group of children get together and tidy up a dirty beach, which used to be very beautiful. It makes us realise how important it is for us to look after our world.

Illustration available on CD ROM   ref: 23

Sunshine Beach

Year three had been doing a topic about the sea. Their classroom was decorated with pictures and paintings. Children had brought souvenirs from the seaside like postcards, fishing nets, buckets and spades, pebbles and shells.

Mrs Martindale, the teacher, asked the children to put their hands up if they had been to the seaside. All but two children put their hands up. Debbie and Luke, the twins, kept their hands down.

"Have you not been to the seaside?" asked Mrs Martindale.

The twins shook their heads.

"Oh dear," said Mrs Martindale, "We'll have to do something about that."

Mrs Martindale decided to arrange a trip to the seaside. That night she sat in her armchair by the fire deciding which seaside town they'd visit. Somewhere different, somewhere the children had never been to. She took out her photograph albums and had a look at her holiday pictures.

"That's it," she said. "We'll go to Sunshine Beach. I haven't been there for nearly five years."

The next day she told the children about the trip to the seaside.

"What's it like at Sunshine Beach?" asked Luke.

"It's the prettiest beach I've ever seen," said Mrs Martindale. "The sand is golden yellow and the beach is long and wide. There are rock pools at the northern end and tall cliffs too. The sea is deep blue, clear, with lots of little fish. There's a short promenade, with pretty flowerbeds and seats where you can sit. It really is a beautiful place."

The children were excited. On the day of the trip they all arrived early. It wasn't long before the coach had arrived at Sunshine Beach. It parked in the car park on the cliff top.

"We'll have to walk from here," said Mrs Martindale. "The only way down to the beach is along the cliffs."

The children followed Mrs Martindale along the cliff top.

"Is it much further?" asked Joanne. "My legs are tired."

"No we're nearly there," said Mrs Martindale. "It will be worth the walk."

They followed her down the path to the beach. Suddenly Mrs Martindale stopped.

"Oh my goodness," said Mrs Martindale. "What on earth has happened to my beautiful beach?"

The children ran onto the concrete

prom and stared in dismay over the rusty railings. A dreadful sight met their eyes. The beach wasn't a golden yellow like Mrs Martindale had described. The beach was a dirty grey colour and greasy oil lapped up on the beach. There were empty cans and bottles strewn all over the sand. There was litter everywhere. Mrs Martindale sat on one of the benches. It was covered in graffiti and someone had carved his/her name on it with a sharp knife. One of the rubbish bins had been turned over and litter was blowing around.

"What a horrible place," said Debbie.

"It used not to be like this," said Mrs Martindale.

"What's happened?" said Luke.

"You tell me," said Mrs Martindale.

"People have spoilt it," said Debbie.

"What are we going to do?" asked Debbie.

"I don't know," said Mrs Martindale shaking her head.

"We could clean it up," said Luke.

"Great idea," shouted the rest of the children.

"But its far too big a job for children," said Mrs Martindale.

"No it's not," said Robert. "My Grandad's got lots of tools in his shed. I'm sure he'd loan them to us."

"And my Mum and Dad have got a

paint shop. I'll be able to get some paint," said Paul.

"And we've plenty of spare bin bags at home," said Joanne.

"Well that's it then, we'll do it," said Mrs Martindale.

The class cheered.

When the class returned from the trip, Mrs Martindale phoned the council offices responsible for Sunshine Beach. A man from the council said that they would give her all the help she needed to return the beach to it's past beauty.

A month later Mrs Martindale and the children returned. The bus was full of the equipment they would need. There were tools of every description, plenty of dustbin liners, litter pickers and paint, tubs and flowers. The children set to work. By four o'clock the beach was transformed. The children sat down on the promenade smiling from head to toe.

"Mrs Martindale, we've done it," said Luke.

"We certainly have," said Mrs Martindale, patting Luke on the head.

"But why are you crying Miss?" asked Debbie

"Oh I don't know, it just brings back memories."

"Memories of what?" asked Debbie.

"Our last holiday together, Mr Martindale and I. We came here when he wasn't well, for a peaceful holiday… It was the last one we had together."

The children looked at Mrs Martindale. She had taken a handkerchief out of her pocket and was wiping her eyes.

"Don't cry," said Debbie. "You should be happy."

"Why?" she asked.

"I'm sure Mr Martindale would have been very pleased had he known you'd come back. Now you'll be able to remember Sunshine Beach and smile. And one day you'll be able to bring another class and if people have made it dirty again, you'll be able to do what we did."

"Perhaps I will," said Mrs Martindale beginning to smile. "Perhaps I will."

WONDERFUL WORLD 4

People often forget what a wonderful world it is that we live in. We watch the seasons come and go but never really appreciate them. Autumn is an enjoyable time for children out doors, especially when the weather is wild and windy. It seems to give children life and energy. It is a time for make-believe and fun.

 Poetry text available on CD ROM   ref: 24

57

A Windy Day

On a windy day,

See how the leaves come swirling down like confetti at a wedding,

Watch them dance in the air like birds flying,

See the branches sway and bend like old men with bad backs,

Watch them fall to the ground and lie there in the road like dead stick men.

Listen to windows creaking and moaning like ghosts on Halloween,

Hear the wind whistling through cracks in the woodwork.

Watch paper fly along the pavements like ghosts with white hoods,

Hear cans rattle and roll like a real jazz band,

Watch bottles smash into walls like a strike at the bowling alley,

See tiles slide down roofs like sledges on a snowy hillside,

See old people stagger left and right as if they're on board a ship in stormy seas,

Watch children fly around the playground fighting the invisible force,

Hear small boys, with their coats flying high racing around the yard like Superheroes,

Watch little girls jump and dance like kites set free from their owners,

On a windy day.

WONDERFUL WORLD 5

The smallest flower, the smallest tree, the smallest child, it doesn't matter how small or insignificant you are, everyone and everything is important. Christians believe God knows everyone and everything and cares for each one just the same.

Illustration available on CD ROM   ref: 25

The Forget-Me-Not

A long time ago the world was full of beautiful flowers. The woods were full of bright colours and their scent could be smelled many a mile away. Children skipped and danced along the footpaths and through the woods admiring them.

In one particular wood lived the Flower Keeper. It was her job to look after the flowers. The Flower Keeper loved her world and looked after it well. In the morning she would fly through the forest tending the flowers and taking care of them. In the evening the Flower Keeper would sit in her favourite spot by the stream and smile.

"I'm going to give every single flower

in this wood a name," she said to a pretty blue flower by the water's edge. "And when I have done this, I will travel on to other woods, until I have named every flower in the world," she said excitedly.

Sometimes the Flower Keeper would be tired and bad tempered when she had had a busy day. The pretty blue flower would listen to her moans and cheer her up when she was feeling sad.

"You're a good friend," said the Flower Keeper. "And when I leave this wood to travel pastures new, I will never forget you."

"Thank you," said the flower, bowing its head rather shyly.

One warm summer evening a young

man came through the wood whistling happily to himself. He called to the Flower Keeper asking for her help.

"I would like some flowers to give to my girlfriend," said the young man. "I'd like some flowers that are like my heart, a deep crimson red."

"How about these?" said the Flower Keeper, pointing to some tall flowers, growing in a sunny spot.

"These are just right," said the boy looking at the flowers with deep red petals and picking some to take to his girlfriend.

"And what is your girlfriend's name?" asked the Flower Keeper.

"She is called Rose, and I love her with all my heart," said the young man.

"Then we shall call this flower rose," said the Flower Keeper and flew off to her resting place by the stream to tell the pretty blue flower.

In autumn lots of people walked through the woods. One day an old man came into the wood. He looked very unhappy.

"What's the matter?" asked the Flower Keeper.

"My wife died recently. I'm so lonely without her," he said.

"Why don't you choose some flowers to remind you of her?" suggested the Flower Keeper.

"What a good idea," said the old man.

"Then tell me about your wife," said the Flower Keeper.

"Well, her name was Violet. She was beautiful and kind. Her perfume smelled so sweet. Our house used to smell of her perfume, but now there is nothing. Violet has gone and I am alone."

The Flower Keeper was sad. She took the old man to a shady spot underneath the old oak tree.

"I think she would have liked these," she said, pointing to some small flowers.

The old man picked a small bunch to take home in memory of his wife.

"And I will call this flower Violet, sweet Violet in memory of your wife," said the Flower Keeper, with a tiny tear in her eye.

One day the Flower Keeper was wakened by the sound of someone running through the forest calling out her name. She flew down onto the forest floor

"What's the matter?" asked the Flower Keeper. "Why are you in such a rush?"

"What am I going to do?" cried the young woman. "The Mayor and Mayoress are coming to open the new nursery school today and we have nothing to give them. I haven't got much time. They'll be here in half an hour and there's so much to do."

The Flower Keeper looked at the young woman.

"Wait here," said the Flower Keeper, "I'll help you. I can give you the ideal present. You need look no further."

The Flower Keeper picked some flowers with pear shaped leaves and russet coloured petals.

"Oh thank you, thank you, they are really beautiful," said the young woman, "but I've got to rush, I'm so busy."

The young lady took the flowers and ran off into the wood.

"But what's your name?" shouted the Flower Keeper.

"Lizzie, Lizzie," came a faint answer in the distance.

"Then I shall call this flower Busy Lizzie," said the Flower Keeper, "because you are a busy Lizzie."

As time went on each flower was given a name, until finally all the flowers had their own names. Sitting in her favourite spot by the stream, the Flower Keeper said to her friend the blue flower,

"I think we should have a party."

"Why is that?" asked the pretty blue flower.

"Well I have named every flower in the wood and I must leave tomorrow," she replied.

"That is a splendid idea," said the

flower, bowing her head slightly, saddened at the thought she was going to lose her best friend.

The Flower Keeper was happy and flew through the wood telling everyone the good news.

"Today, I am pleased to announce that every flower has its own name," she called out to the woodland folk. "Let's have a party!" she shouted excitedly.

The woodland folk cheered and began to sing and dance. The Flower Keeper flew through the forest looking at her beautiful world. Suddenly, she heard sobbing. She followed the sound to the stream and there by the riverbank she saw a flower. It had slender spoon shaped leaves and beautiful blue petals, the colour of a summer sky. Just then she realised this was her loyal friend the blue flower, but she was crying.

"Why are you crying?" asked the Flower keeper.

"Every flower has a name, but not I," she sobbed. "You have forgotten me."

"You are mistaken said the Flower Keeper. "How could I forget you? You are my friend and you are also one of the most beautiful flowers in the wood. Don't cry, you already have a name."

The pretty blue flower lifted its head slowly.

"I have called you Forget-Me-Not," said the Flower Keeper. "How could anyone possibly forget a good friend like you?"

"Thank you," said the flower. "Thank you for giving me such a wonderful name."

WONDERFUL WORLD 6

We often do not always realise just how lucky we are. Sometimes we are not happy with the way we look. At other times, we take things like our health for granted. Sometimes we moan because we're not the neatest worker, or because we can't play the recorder properly, or because we never win races. However, we should be grateful for even the simplest things such as we have arms and legs that work properly and enable us to have so much fun. 'Fun at the Seaside', is a story about a girl who is disabled. Staying seated the children can join in the actions in the story. The story will show them how much we use our hands and how they give us so much pleasure.

Illustration available on
CD ROM   ref: 26

Fun at the Seaside

Angela loved the seaside. She loved going there with her family on hot summer days when the sun was shining and the sky was blue. She'd sit on the sand and build sand castles. She'd dig a moat with her spade. Dad would fetch some water in a bucket and she'd tip it into the moat. She'd put a flag on the biggest sandcastle.

Sometimes she would collect seashells. She would pick up shells of different shapes and sizes to decorate the sides of the sand castle so that they looked like windows and doors. She'd put the prettiest ones in her bucket full of water and wash the sand away so they looked like shiny jewels.

Sometimes she would sit on a stone by a small rock pool. She'd get her net and put it into the water. She'd catch tiny crabs and put them into her bucket. Sometimes she'd see little fish. She'd put her hands in the water and feel them swim across her hand. If she

were quick enough she'd catch one and put it in a jam jar.

At lunchtime they'd have a picnic. She liked finger teacakes filled with ham. She'd eat one in just three bites. She would drink lemonade from a bottle with a long straw. Then Dad would go to the ice cream van. He'd bring her a '99'. She'd take out the flake and eat that first. Then she'd lick all the ice cream until it disappeared inside the cone. She'd bite a hole in the bottom of the cone and suck the ice cream.

Angela enjoyed the seaside; so much so, it didn't even seem to matter that she was unable to walk. It didn't matter if Dad had to carry her back to the car or if she'd have to sit in her wheel chair. She had her hands after all, and where would she be without them.

MAGIC 1

'Bobby's Wish' tells the story of a boy who makes a wish. However, the wish makes him very unhappy. It makes us realise that things we think will make us really happy are not always the things that actually do.

 Illustration available on CD ROM   ref: 27

Bobby's Wish

On Monday Bobby had a bad day at

school. The Head teacher told him off for pushing in the assembly line. The secretary told him off for forgetting his dinner money. The teacher told him off for doing messy work. At dinnertime he was sent inside by the dinner ladies for pushing someone over in the yard. Finally, he was told off again by his teacher for being noisy and silly during story time. It had been a dreadful day. Bobby was still in a bad mood going to school on Tuesday morning.

"I hate school," he said. "You get told off for everything. I wish… I wish that there weren't any adults or children in school at all. It would be much more fun."

Bobby walked into the classroom. There was nobody there. It was really quiet; no teacher; no children.

"Great!" he shouted, running around the room. "My wish has come true."

He got all the toys out of the box and spread them out on the carpet.

"I can play all day," he laughed.

But after a while he got bored.

"It's not much fun playing on your own," he said.

He decided to do a few sums in his book. He managed the first few but then he got stuck. He put his hand up, that's what he usually did when he was stuck. But then he remembered the teacher wasn't there.

He decided to draw a picture and got out the best paper and felt tip pens but he couldn't think what to draw.

"If my teacher was here she'd give me lots of ideas," he grumbled.

But unfortunately the room was empty. He went into the hall to see if it was time for assembly. He was looking forward to singing a song. But there was nobody there.

Sadly, he went back into the classroom and sat on the floor. He looked up at the clock. He couldn't tell the time yet. He hadn't listened in class the other day when the teacher had been explaining it all.

"I know what," he said, "I'll go and read to Mrs Robinson."

He picked up his reading book, and went out into the corridor where she usually sat. But she wasn't there. The corridor was empty. He was hungry and thirsty.

"It must be milk time," he said. But, of course, the milk monitors hadn't been and so there was no milk. Bobby went out into the yard.

"Great," he said. "The whole yard to myself."

But he soon got fed up. There was no one to play tig with or pretend to be monsters with. Sadly, he went back into the classroom.

"I'll see if dinner's ready," he said, and went into the hall.

The cook wasn't there or the dinner ladies and there was no food. "Where is everyone?" he shouted.

He ran across the hall but he tripped and went head over heels into the wall.

"Ouch," he said, looking down at his knee. It was grazed and bleeding a little bit. "I'll go and ask the Secretary for a plaster," he said, hobbling to the door.

He knocked several times but there was no answer. He sat down on the chair and began to cry.

"I wish… I wish that everyone would come back," he said, feeling very sorry for himself.

Then he heard the front door open and footsteps coming towards him.

"What's the matter Bobby?" said the voice.

Bobby looked up. It was the Head teacher.

"You're very early," she said. "It's only half past eight."

Bobby couldn't understand it at all. He looked at his knee. It wasn't grazed. That was strange.

"Go out into the yard until the bell goes," she said, "and when you come in, tell your teacher that if the class are good today I'll come and read them a story this afternoon."

"Thank you Miss," said Bobby, walking to the door.

He walked onto the yard and then looked through the classroom window. His teacher was there at her desk. The nursery nurses were there too.

"I must have been dreaming," he said walking into the classroom when the bell rang. "I think I'll be good today. After all, I don't want to spend the day on my own again," he said taking his seat and waiting quietly for the teacher.

64

MAGIC 2

Sometimes we don't always realise the impression we give to other people. Sometimes it takes a harsh word or action to make us realise and finally do something to improve the situation.

 Illustration available on CD ROM   ref: 28

Roger's Garden

Roger was a gnome. He lived in a little house all on his own at the edge of the wood. Roger didn't have any friends because he was fat and lazy. He was also very untidy. You should have seen his house. It was a disgrace and his garden was even worse. On sunny days he would sit outside on his bench eating crisps and drinking pop. He'd drop the empty crisp packets on the grass and throw the cans at any animal that came by. The garden was full of broken bottles, old newspapers, sweet wrappers, empty tin cans and rotting food.

One morning while Roger was having his breakfast he heard a lot of noise outside his front window. He went outside to see what was going on.

"What's happening?" he asked.

"The Queen is coming," shouted Thomas, one of the younger gnomes.

Roger looked along the lane. He could see a gold carriage pulled by four white mice. All the gnomes stood at the roadside and waved. The carriage stopped outside Roger's house. A gnome in a smart blue suit jumped off the carriage. He gave out posters to the watching gnomes. He gave one to Roger.

"What does it say?" asked Roger who couldn't be bothered to read his poster.

"It's a competition," said Peter, "for the tidiest garden."

"Oh," said Roger, "perhaps I'll enter."

All the other gnomes looked at him and laughed.

"You'll never win," they said.

"Why not?" said Roger

"Yours is the worst garden in the whole land," one gnome replied.

Roger walked sadly up the garden path. He looked around the garden. They were quite right. It was a mess.

He went inside and made himself a cup of tea. How could he win? He just didn't know. What would he do? Where would he start?

The next morning Roger got up early. All the gnomes were fast asleep in their beds. He stood at the back door and looked at his messy garden. He noticed a sign in the garden that he hadn't seen before. He looked at it closely. It said

'THE UGLIEST GARDEN
IN GNOME LAND'

65

Roger began to cry. He ran down the path and into the wood, tears streaming down his chubby cheeks. He went deep into the wood where the trees were tall and no sun shone through. He came upon a clearing where there was a well. He sat down by the well and cried and cried until he had no tears left. Eventually he fell asleep. He woke up at the sound of someone shouting.

Roger listened. The voice was coming from inside the well.

"Help," called the voice again.

Roger stood up and leaned over to look into the well.

"Help me," said the voice. "I've fallen down the well and I can't get out."

"Oh dear," said Roger. "Don't worry, I'll help you."

Roger found a bucket and lowered it into the well. He pulled it up very carefully and a tiny fairy jumped out.

"Thank you," said the fairy. "That was a kind thing to do."

The fairy noticed that Roger had been crying.

"What's the matter?" she asked, "why are you so sad?"

Roger told her about the tidiest garden competition.

"I have an idea," said the fairy. "Tonight, when the sun has set, go into the garden and wait for me. I will help you."

"But I won't be able to see," said Roger, "It will be too dark."

"Wait and see," chuckled the fairy.

Suddenly the sun appeared between the trees and lit up the dark wood and in the twinkling of an eye, the fairy had gone.

Roger ran home. That night when the sun had gone down and all the other gnomes had gone to bed, Roger crept into the garden. He looked around. And there in the middle of the garden was a bright light, a silver circle. It shone down on his messy garden. What a disgrace it was, full of empty cans and tins.

"I'll tidy these up before the fairy comes," he said.

He set to work and in no time at all it was done. He went to bed tired but happy.

The next night when all the gnomes had gone to bed Roger went into the garden. The bright light was in a different place, and that too was a real mess. There was a broken bottle.

"I can't leave all this broken glass around," said Roger, "The fairy might cut herself."

He set to work and tidied it up.

On the fifth night Roger went out into the garden. The light shone down on a pile of sweet wrappers and crisp packets.

"I'll sweep these up before the fairy comes," he said.

Roger set to work. Afterwards he sat down for a rest.

"I can't understand it," he said. "I thought that fairy was going to help me. It's the competition tomorrow. I'll never win."

Roger went inside a very unhappy gnome. He woke up with the sound of cheering. No doubt the Queen had arrived. She was probably giving out the prize to the gnome with the best garden. Roger hid under the covers. Then there was a loud knock at the door.

"Roger, get up," said the voice. "The Queen is here."

Roger got dressed quickly and ran down stairs. He opened the front door. Everyone began to cheer.

"The winner is Roger," said the Queen's helper.

The Queen got down from her carriage and presented Roger with his prize.

"You must be mistaken," said Roger. "I haven't got the best garden."

"But you have," said the Queen. "Take a look around you."

Roger looked at his garden and then rubbed his eyes. He couldn't believe it. His garden was the tidiest in the whole land. Everyone clapped and cheered.

Later on that day when the sun had set Roger went outside and sat on his bench in the garden. Suddenly the fairy appeared.

"Where have you been? You promised to help me," said Roger.

"I did," said the fairy. "I was with you every night."

"But I didn't see you once," said Roger.

"I shone my light to help you," said the fairy. "I am the moon fairy, that was my light you saw in the garden."

And with that she shot up into the sky.

Roger looked up at the sky. He could see the moon. It was shining down on his beautiful garden. So the moon fairy had helped him after all. She guided him. Without her light he wouldn't have won the competition.

"Thank you Moon Fairy, thank you so much," said Roger looking at his beautiful garden.

MAGIC 3

'Do you believe in Leprechauns?' tells the story of a naughty, selfish boy. When he goes on holiday to Ireland he becomes a better person after a somewhat frightening experience with a leprechaun.

 Illustration available on CD ROM   ref: 29

Do you believe in Leprechauns?

"We're going on holiday to Ireland," said Tom to his Grandma.

"Well you'd better watch out," said Grandma.

"What for?" asked Tom.

"Leprechauns. They're the little people. They play tricks on people, especially naughty children," said Grandma.

"I don't believe in leprechauns," said Tom.

"Well, you'd better behave yourself then," she said.

But Tom wasn't listening, he was thinking about the big boat they'd be travelling on across the sea to Ireland.

Tom slept most of the overnight crossing from Holyhead to Dublin. When he woke up they had arrived at Auntie Flo's. Tom had never met Auntie Flo.

"Be nice to her," said Mum. "She's got arthritis."

Tom grunted. Why was it you always had to be nice to relatives?

Auntie Flo was really old. Her hands were withered like an old tree stump. She held a walking stick in her hand.

Auntie Flo had made some Irish stew. Tom was starving. He pushed an enormous spoonful into his mouth.

"Tom! Manners!" said his mother.

Tom pulled a face and carried on eating. His plate was empty in no time at all. Tom was just about to lick his plate when his father looked at him.

"Don't you dare," said his father.

Tom burped, "What's for pudding?"

"Well, I've made some barm brack," said Auntie Flo, pointing to what looked like a currant loaf. "I always bake one at this time of year. I made it specially for you."

Tom took a huge bite.

"Ugh!" he said, spitting out the currants. "It's horrible!"

Dad was cross and sent Tom to bed. Tom peered through the curtains. Across the road there was a patch of green land and in the middle stood a circle of tall trees. Tom could see a light flickering. It darted among the trees and came towards him getting bigger and brighter by the second then stopped across the road. Tom could see a little man holding a lantern dressed in strange clothes and wearing a pointed hat. Tom laughed and pulled a face at him. The little man looked up at the room. He shook his fist at Tom. Tom stuck his tongue out then jumped back into bed quickly.

For a while Tom lay there in the darkness thinking about the funny little man. Then he remembered what his grandma had told him. He was to watch out for leprechauns. But that was silly. Eleven-year-old boys didn't believe in all that nonsense.

At breakfast Tom slurped his cornflakes.

"What are we going to do today?" asked Tom.

"Why don't you visit Blarney Castle," said Auntie Flo, a twinkle in her eyes. People come from all over the world to see it. They climb to the top and then kiss the Blarney stone."

"Yuck!" said Tom.

"You'll like the castle Tom," she said. "There's the fairy wood and the fairy steps. Mind you, you'd better watch out for the leprechauns, they're fearsome little chaps," she said, winking at Tom's mum. "They're always on the lookout for mischievous boys!"

"I don't believe in all that stuff," said Tom. "It's for kids."

After lunch, Auntie Flo had a nap.

Mum, Dad and Tom went to the castle. Tom ran on ahead.

"Come back!" called Mum, but Tom was gone.

He followed the winding lane to the castle. The tower was really high and set on a small hill. Tom climbed the narrow steps puffing and panting with each step. There were a few people at the top of the castle. They were standing at one end watching a man lie down on his back to kiss the Blarney stone.

"Yuck!" shouted Tom, "I'm not kissing a stone."

He ran down the steps nearly crushing an old lady who was making her way up. He hid behind a tree and although

69

he heard his parents calling he ignored them.

"Just wait till I find him," said Dad angrily. "He's in serious trouble!"

Tom laughed and ran off into the grounds. He followed a path over the bridge and noticed a sign in front of him:

To The Fairy Steps
KEEP TO THE PATH!

Tom left the footpath and strayed into the wood. Suddenly a fierce breeze sprang up from nowhere and it began to rain. The wind began to pull at his hair and bite into his skin. A shiver ran down his spine. Then suddenly he heard the crunch of leaves behind him and footsteps moving rather quickly. He turned to see a flash of red disappear behind a tree. Tom ran as fast as he could to the footpath. It wound its way down a hill to the brook. He followed the path and stopped when he got to a large sign.

"The wishing steps – walk to the top with your eyes shut. Make a wish and it will come true."

The wishing steps were inside a tunnel. It was damp and cold inside and water dripped from the roof. The further he went, the longer the tunnel became. Tom was frightened. He forgot about making a wish and ran as fast as he could. He could see daylight ahead and a figure at the entrance.

The figure looked at Tom and laughed. It was that horrible little man Tom had seen the night before! The little man ran away.

Tom looked around. He wasn't sure which way to go. Then he saw a signpost. It had three signs on it. They all said – "WAY OUT!" Tom followed the path to the left, which wound its way up the hill. It stopped in front of an old oak tree. It was a dead end. Tom was soaking wet and his trainers squeaked and squelched. He sat down underneath the tree his heart pounding. He shivered and wrapped his arms around his chest. As the tears began to fall down his cheeks, the autumn leaves in the oak tree began to fall around him. They covered him like a thick blanket.

"Tom," said a familiar voice, "How are you feeling?"

Tom opened his eyes slowly. He was in bed at Auntie Flo's.

"What happened?" he asked.

"You fell and banged your head," said Auntie Flo.

"But something happened in the woods. I'm sure I saw a leprechaun. Do you believe in leprechauns Auntie Flo?"

"No, that's a load of old nonsense," she said. "Now drink this cocoa, it will make you feel better.

Auntie Flo smiled and went

downstairs. Tom looked out of the window. A flash of red in front of the trees across the road made him blink. He sat upright to get a better look. He could see the same little man he thought he'd seen yesterday. But the little man didn't look angry any more, he was waving. Tom watched as the little man ran back into the trees.

"Leprechauns?" thought Tom. "Yes, I believe in leprechauns."

ALL KINDS OF CHILDREN 1

Everyone knows a bully. Bullies upset other children. They often pick on children younger and weaker than themselves. Billy the Bully is a poem about a bully and how he got his just desserts.

 Poetry text available on CD ROM   ref: 30

Billy the Bully

Billy was a bully
    The worst in all the school,
He terrorised the children
And broke all of the rules.
Billy was a big lad
Much bigger than the rest,
The staff didn't know what to do
    with him

He really was a pest.
He teased some of the children.
Laughed and called them names,
He'd kick and knock them over
And not let them play in games.
The children were so frightened
They didn't know what to do,
They said, "Billy you're a bully
We've had enough of you."

Then a dreadful thing happened
When the children went to the farm,
They saw a large bull in the
    field nearby
Said Bill, "I'll come to no harm."
Billy jumped right over the fence
Saying, "A bull fighter I will be,
Just look at that bull, what a
    softy he is
I'm sure he's frightened of me."

Billy waved his red hanky
He didn't really care,
The bull took one look and lowered
    his horns
Then flung him right in the air.
The children watched in amazement
As Billy flew up to the moon
That was the last time they saw him
And it certainly wasn't too soon.

71

ALL KINDS OF CHILDREN 2

'Terry No Chance' tells us the story of a boy who was always in trouble. Because of his reputation he had no friends until one day he did something very brave. The story tells us to forgive people and give them a second chance; no matter what awful things they have done in the past.

 Illustration available on CD ROM   ref: 31

Terry No Chance

Once there was a boy called Terry No Chance. That was his nickname; his real name was Terry Jones. He was given his nickname after only a few months at school. When Terry was in the first class at school he was very naughty. When the children were playing nicely together, Terry would come up to them and knock over their Lego towers or spill the paint pots. He even threw sand over the other children when they were playing in the sand pit. Then Terry would go up to the children and say, "Can I play?"

"No chance!" they'd reply and move away. Every time he asked he got the same reply.

When he went into the Juniors, he was just as bad. He would spoil children's work, steal their lunches and fight with the other boys.

"Can I play?" he'd ask the other boys. "No chance," they'd reply and run away. Terry was so naughty the other children would shout his name on the yard. "Terry No Chance, Terry No Chance!"

Of course, Terry didn't have a friend in the world, not one. Until one day everything changed.

By this time, Terry was in Year 6. He wasn't really naughty any more, but he still had no friends. The children couldn't forget all the horrible things he'd done. He walked to school every day on his own, because no one would walk with him. One morning he was walking to school when he heard shouting. He saw two big lads teasing a much smaller girl. It was Jennifer. She was in Year 3, but she was really small; she still looked like an infant child.

"What's going on?" said Terry.

"Mind your own business," said one of the lads, who was at least three years older than Terry.

The two boys were playing catch with the little girl's sandwich box. Most children would have been afraid because the two lads were at High School.

"Leave her alone," shouted Terry.

"Or else, what'll you do?" shouted the tallest lad.

72

"Give it back," shouted Terry.

"Come and get it," said the other lad.

Terry rushed up to the boy holding the sandwich box and snatched it from him.

"Run!" he shouted to Jennifer.

Jennifer ran off along the back road to school.

No one is quite sure what happened next. But a few minutes later the Deputy Headteacher was seen running down to where the incident had happened. Terry was lying on the ground, covered in dirt, a graze on his face. However, he was still holding on to the sandwich box. The two older boys were nowhere to be seen.

In assembly the next morning, the Headteacher told everyone that they had a very brave boy in the school.

The children looked around wondering who it could be. The Headteacher asked the person to come out to the front. Everyone was surprised when Terry stood up and walked to the front. The children clapped when the headteacher told them the story. When the children went back to class they were very quiet. They looked very sad.

"What's the matter with you all?" asked the teacher.

Thomas put his hand up. "We're very sorry," he said.

"What for?" asked the teacher.

"We never gave him a chance," said Thomas.

All the children looked at Terry.

"We're sorry," they all said.

"That's okay," said Terry quietly.

"You can play football with us at playtime," said Thomas.

"Thanks," said Terry. "I'd like that."

ALL KINDS OF CHILDREN 3

Sometimes people are faced with a difficult task. It may be so difficult that they want to give up without trying. 'The Competition' tells us about a boy who didn't have any confidence. Gradually he learned to believe in himself and realised that he could achieve what he wanted.

Illustration available on
CD ROM   ref: 32

The Competition

On the Friday before the summer holidays the Headteacher at St. Peter's school called all the children into the hall.

"We're going to have a family fun run after the summer holidays," he said. "The winning team will receive a signed football from Dunston United."

The children gasped. Dunston United were top of the Premier League.

"Wow!" said Freddie, a boy in Year Five.

"What a prize," said Lennie, the boy sitting next to him.

The children took letters home to show their parents. The next day was Saturday, the first day of the holidays. Freddie was sitting on the pavement throwing stones down the grate when Lennie went past on his bike.

"Don't bother entering the fun run," said Lennie. "My dad says we're going to win."

He did a wheelie on his bike and rode off down the street.

That night Freddie's family sat around the tea table. Dad had the letter on the table.

"Would you like to enter the Fun Run?" asked Dad.

"I don't know," said Freddie. "I saw Lennie today. He said that he was going to win."

"And how do you know that?" asked Dad.

"Because his Dad said so," said Freddie. "Lennie's in Red Star Running Team and his Dad's the trainer. We've no chance."

"Oh well then," said Dad, folding the piece of paper up and putting it on the table. "It looks like Lennie will get the signed football then."

Freddie picked up the letter. He'd love to win that ball. But there was no chance.

"We couldn't beat them," said Freddie.

"Oh yes we could," said Dad.

"How?" asked Freddie.

"We'll have to get fit," replied his Dad. "All of us."

"How?"

"What we need is an action plan," said Dad.

"Ugh!" said Freddie. "I don't like the sound of that."

"Number one," said Dad. "Good food."

"Does that mean no chocolates or cream buns?" asked Freddie.

"That's right," said Dad. "And number two, plenty of exercise."

"Does that mean I have to walk to school?" asked Freddie.

"Yes."

"And number three?" asked Freddie.

"Bed early," said Dad.

"How early?" asked Freddie.

"Very early," replied Dad.

"Ugh!" replied Freddie. "I think I've changed my mind."

"But what about the signed football?" said Dad. "You don't want Lennie to win it, do you?"

Lennie won everything. It would be great if he could win something for once. A signed football was just what he'd always wanted, but, all that hard work! Could they do it?

The next six weeks were the worst six weeks of Freddie's life. They'd run up to the moors every night and tried to do it faster each time.

"I can't go on," said Freddie sitting down on a stone during one of their runs.

"You can't give up," said Dad. "We're in this together."

"But I'm tired and my legs ache," cried Freddie.

Dad helped him to his feet.

"We can do it," said Dad. "You've got to believe in yourself."

That night the family sat down at the tea table.

"I hate cauliflower and carrots," said Freddie picking at his food.

"But they're good for you, they'll make you strong," said Mum

"But I don't want to be strong," said Freddie. "I want a Big Mac and Fries and chocolate cake for afters, and a glass of Coke and some sweets."

"But if you eat that kind of thing, you won't have the energy to run and we'll lose."

"I don't care," said Freddie. "I don't care."

"Oh yes you do," said Dad. "You don't want Lennie to win the football do you?"

"No, of course I don't," said Freddie. "But I can't do this any more. I'm tired and hungry and fed up."

75

"We can't give up now. We can do it," said Mum. "I know it's hard work, but it will be worth it in the end.

"Six weeks later Freddie was the fittest he'd ever been. The day before the race while Freddie was having his lunch Lennie came up behind him and nudged him in the back.

"You've no chance tomorrow," said Lennie. "My Dad says we're going to win the football."

"Not if I can help it," said Freddie.

"We'll soon see," said Lennie, giving him another thump.

After school, Freddie decided to go for one more run on the moors. He'd just reached the top of Crag Moor when he heard a woman shouting. He ran to where the voice was coming from. He saw a lady on her knees. She was stroking the head of a man who lay by her side.

"What's the matter?" asked Freddie.

"My husband's had a heart attack. Get help."

Freddie ran across the moor faster than he'd ever been before. He ran so fast he fell over a large stone.

"Ouch!" he said, getting back to his feet.

He didn't stop until he reached the nearest telephone box where he dialled 999. In minutes the ambulance had arrived and taken the man to hospital.

Freddie ran into the house collapsing in a heap on the settee. His ankle throbbed so much he cried.

The next day was the race. Freddie stayed at home. His foot was so badly swollen he couldn't put any weight on it. The competition took place and Lennie's family won.

At five o' clock there was a knock on the door. It was Lennie. He was carrying a plastic bag.

"I'm sorry about your foot," said Lennie. "You would have won it by miles."

Freddie looked at his badly swollen foot and shrugged.

"I'm sorry I've been so mean to you. Can we be mates?" asked Lennie, holding out his hand.

"Okay," said Freddie shaking his hand. "Are you going to the match on Saturday?"

"Yes, my Dad's got tickets," said Lennie.

"I wish I was going," said Freddie.

"I think you might be," said Lennie.

"What do you mean?" asked Freddie.

Just then Dad walked through the door.

"This is for you," said Dad, giving Freddie an envelope.

Freddie opened the envelope. Inside was a ticket.

"A ticket for the match," shouted Freddie.

"And that's not all," said Dad. "You're going to be the mascot."

"What?" shouted Freddie.

"That man you saved on the moors is Harry Bates."

"Harry Bates!" said Freddie. "The chairman of Dunston United?"

"Yes, that's right, the chairman of Dunston United," said Dad.

"Wow," said Freddie.

"He's so grateful for what you did, he wants you to be the mascot at next Saturday's home match. They're going to present you with a signed ball as well," said Dad.

"It looks like you'll be going to the match after all," said Lennie.

"Wow!" shouted Freddie. "That's the best prize ever."

"See you next Saturday then," said Lennie, waving goodbye.

"Yeah, see you then," smiled Freddie, an enormous grin all over his face. "See you at the match."

ALL KINDS OF CHILDREN 4

Sometimes when you are playing, a stray ball might hit you, or someone may bump into you. Most of the time it is an accident. As long as the person says sorry, you should accept it as an accident.

Illustration available on CD ROM   ref: 33

Accidents Can Happen

It snowed all night. In the morning the ground was covered with a thick white carpet. Jack couldn't wait to get to school. He was thinking about all the fun he was going to have. When he got there the yard was full of excited children. Some of the younger ones were making snowmen and some were making slides. There were no teachers about. Suddenly a snowball flew through the air.

"I bet I can make mine go further," shouted a boy's voice.

"No chance," said another boy.

Then a competition began between the boys in Year 6 as to who could throw a snowball the furthest. The Year 6 boys began making snowballs. Jack joined in the fun. He was a big lad and his snowball went a long way.

"Terrific throw," shouted one of the boys.

Stephen, a younger boy picked up some snow and made several snowballs. He threw them in all directions, only just missing a group of girls making a snowman.

"Stephen you're getting in the way," said one of the boys from Year 6. "Go and play somewhere else."

Stephen went to the other end of the yard. He made a few more snowballs and began throwing them towards the line of Year 6 boys. He didn't throw them very far.

"My sister could throw further than that," said one of the Year 6 boys, looking Stephen in the eye.

Some of the Year 6 boys laughed.

Stephen pulled a face. He began making the largest snowball you'd ever seen.

"Just wait till I throw this one," he said.

The Year 6 boys carried on their competition at the other end of the yard, making sure they didn't hit anyone.

It was nearly time for the bell. Jack decided to have one more go. The snow had started melting. He could see gravel appearing. Carefully he picked up some snow and made it into a ball.

"Go on Jack," shouted one of the boys. "See if you can reach the other side of the yard."

Jack took a run up and then threw the snowball as hard as he could. It flew through the air like a meteorite. The children cheered excitedly. Then it began to drop. There was a gasp from the children as the snowball hit Stephen on the head. He'd just finished making an enormous snowball and

had turned around to show everyone how big it was.

"Ouch!" he shouted, rubbing his head. Jack and a few of the other boys ran over to him.

"Are you all right?" asked Jack. "I didn't mean it. It was an accident."

"It's okay," said Stephen getting up and brushing the snow off his head.

"Mr Brown's coming," shouted one of the children.

"What's going on?" asked the teacher. "Get inside at once. I'll speak to you both in a minute."

All the children went inside. Mr Brown went into the hall. The two boys were waiting there for him. The teacher listened to the story. He looked at Stephen's head. There was no bruising and he looked fine.

"Okay, I believe it was an accident," said Mr Brown. "But don't throw snowballs anymore. You could hurt somebody."

The boys nodded their heads and went back to their classrooms. Stephen forgot about his head until home time. Then on the way out of school he heard a Year 6 boy talking to another boy.

"They got done off Mr Brown for throwing snowballs," said one of the boys.

Stephen was angry. He didn't want others thinking he had done anything wrong. "Just wait till I get home. I'll tell my Dad that it was all Jack's fault, and that he hit me on purpose."

The next day, Stephen didn't come to school. One of the boys in Year 6 asked Stephen's younger brother where he was.

"He's in bed with a bandage on his head," said Thomas, Stephen's younger brother. "Jack threw a snowball with a stone in the middle of it. Stephen said that Jack did it on purpose and that the boys in Year 6 are bullying him."

The story spread all over the school. Soon the headmaster heard all about it. He called Jack to his room. Jack was really frightened. He stood outside

the Headteacher's office trembling. He felt like crying. It was an accident, it really was. Jack knocked on the door.

"Come in," said a deep voice.

Jack went inside.

The Headteacher looked up from behind his desk.

"Did you put a stone in the middle of the snowball and try to hit Stephen with it?" he asked.

"No," said Jack, quite frightened. "We were just playing. I didn't mean to hurt him. We were having a competition to see who could throw a snowball the furthest."

"Right," said the Headteacher. "Go and wait outside."

The Headteacher called Mr Brown, the teacher, to his room.

"Do you think that Jack did it on purpose?"

"No," said the teacher. "He's not that kind of boy. I'm sure it was an accident. I've spoken to the other boys about it. They say it was an accident too."

The next morning the Headmaster came into assembly. He told the children about a boy who nearly got another boy into trouble by telling lies. The Headmaster told the children that accidents could happen.

"They happen all the time," he said,

"especially at school. You may be playing tig and someone might accidentally pull the hood on your coat and it rips. Don't go home and tell your mum they did it on purpose, you could get that person into terrible trouble. You may be playing football in the yard and someone might tackle you and catch your leg so that you fall over. They say they are sorry and that they didn't mean to do it. So don't go and tell your teacher that they did it on purpose. Accidents happen. If you tell lies, you could make matters worse than they already are."

Stephen bowed his head in shame. The headmaster was right, it had been an accident.

ALL KINDS OF CHILDREN 5

Most of us don't realise how lucky we are. We are healthy and have the use of all our senses, so that when we go to school we can learn to the best of our ability. However, some people don't always use their senses and this often leads to problems just like the boy in the story 'Stop, Look, Listen'.

 Illustration available on CD ROM   ref: 34

Stop, Look, Listen

John was eleven years old. He was in Year 6 at school. He drove the teachers to despair. And why was that? It was because he never thought about what he was doing. He always seemed to be day- dreaming.

"What did I say?" asked the teacher, who knew that John hadn't been listening.

"Pardon?" said John who hadn't been concentrating. He'd been thinking about the football match he'd seen on TV the night before.

"John, come and tidy your bed," said his mother.

John never heard her; he was either watching TV or playing on his computer.

John's parents went to talk to his teacher.

"What are we going to do about him?" they asked.

"I don't know. We've tried everything. He never looks or listens," the teacher replied, shaking her head.

One morning the teacher decided to give the children a maths test from their new book. John was fiddling with a small toy on his desk. He wasn't listening at all.

"Right," said the teacher. "Turn to page forty two in your books. I want you to do all the sums on that page. When you've finished stay in your place until the bell goes. There is to be no talking."

The children opened their books.

"Easy," said John to the girl next to him. "Page four and two, we've done these before."

And just before the girl could tell him they were the wrong pages the teacher called out.

"You may begin now."

The room went silent.

"Great," thought John. "Tens and units, addition. We did those in Year 3."

In ten minutes John had finished. He took a small toy out of his pencil case and played with it until the bell rang. At the end of the test, the teacher walked around the classroom collecting in the children's work. She picked up John's piece of paper.

"What's this?" she asked.

"Page four and two," said John.

All the children laughed.

"Four and two!" shouted the teacher. "Do you ever listen? I said forty two!"

The children laughed again. John laughed too.

"I don't think it's very funny," said the teacher. "In fact, you're not going to find it very funny either. You're going to stay in all dinnertime and do the right page.

She gave him the book and opened it at the right page.

John looked at the book and pulled a funny face.

"Oh no! Page forty-two, division! I can't do these," said John.

"And why is that?" asked the teacher.

"I don't know," said John.

"I'll tell you why you can't do division," she replied. "It's because you don't listen."

"Pardon," said John, who had been looking out of the window.

"I said you never listen," replied the teacher. "But today is the day you start listening. Now get on with the test. Everyone else can go out to play."

John picked up his pencil and sighed. He looked at the page of sums. They were so difficult. If only he'd listened when the teacher had taught the class how to do them.

The teacher called him to her desk.

"This time I'll help you," she said.

"But it's the last time. From now on you've got to learn to look and listen."

John picked up his books and walked to the front. He could see the boys enjoying a great game of football outside in the sunshine. Yes, she was right. It was about time he listened.

ALL KINDS OF CHILDREN 6

Sometimes people don't listen to warnings and as a result have to pay the consequences. Often, adults tell children not to do things. However, children don't always appreciate what they are saying and go ahead regardless. 'Look But Don't Touch', tells children what can happen when they don't take notice of good advice.

 Illustration available on CD ROM   ref: 35

Look But Don't Touch

The children in Miss Peterson's class were doing a topic on the Second World War. They'd learned lots of things. They'd read books, drawn pictures, had visitors in to tell them all about it, but the best part was the day when they made a museum.

"I'd like you to bring in some things to do with the war," said Miss Peterson, "But don't worry if you can't find anything, I'll ring the museum to see what they have on loan."

The following Monday, the children couldn't wait to get to school. It was going to be fun. They covered their desks with paper and set out everything they'd brought. There were all sorts of things, old photos, money, coins, ration books and war medals but best of all there was a gas mask. Miss Peterson had borrowed it from the local museum. It was still in the box and looked brand new. Everyone crowded round to have a look.

"You can look," said Miss Peterson quite sternly, "but you must not touch."

And when Miss Peterson said you couldn't touch, she meant it. The children stared at it all morning, but no one dared pick it up.

When the bell rang the children rushed out to play. Wayne and Luke stayed behind to look at the exhibits. They were best of friends and went everywhere together. They were the most unlikely twosome. Wayne was tall and broad with a wide grin and rosy cheeks. He'd never had a day off school in his whole life and yet he never wore a vest and even played out in the pouring rain without a coat. Luke on the other hand was pale and thin. He'd been off school with mumps, measles, coughs, bronchitis and even asthma and yet he wore a vest, right through the summer too.

Luke was the smallest in the class and everyone called him Little Luke, everyone except Wayne who never called him names. Wayne looked after him. In return, Luke stopped Wayne from getting up to mischief; well, most of the time.

They looked at the gas mask in the box.

"I wonder what it would be like to wear one during the war?" said Wayne looking at it closely.

"My Grandad said it was frightening," said Luke.

"I'd love to take it out of its box," said Wayne excitedly.

"Miss said you've not to touch it," whispered Luke.

"Why not?" said Wayne with that mischievous look in his eyes.

"Because Miss said so," replied Luke beginning to feel nervous.

"I'm sure just one little look won't hurt," said Wayne reaching out to the box and picking it up.

"You shouldn't," said Luke. "Wait till after play. Miss will show it to us then."

But Wayne had already taken it out of the box. He unravelled the straps and had just put it over Luke's head when he heard footsteps and a familiar voice.

"Wayne Smith, what did I tell you?" said Miss Peterson, appearing at the classroom door.

"Er…. not to touch, Miss," said Wayne.

"Luke, take off that gas mask at once," she said sternly.

Wayne tried to pull it off, but the straps got tangled around Luke's ears.

"It won't come off Miss. It's stuck!" said Wayne.

"Take it off now," said Miss Peterson sharply.

Wayne pulled hard but it wouldn't budge.

"It looks like we'll have to send Luke back to the museum as well as the gas mask," said Wayne not realising the seriousness of the situation. "He can be one of the exhibits!"

"That's not funny," said Miss Peterson, hurrying across the classroom.

Wayne tried again.

"Ouch!" shouted Luke trying to untangle the straps.

"Stop messing about," said Miss Peterson, beginning to sound angry

But it really is stuck, Miss," said Wayne again, beginning to notice the frightened look in his friend's eyes.

Then the rest of the children appeared from the yard. Seeing the gas mask for real out of its box they crowded round, some giggling, some pulling funny faces. Luke was pulling frantically at the straps around his head.

"I... can't... breathe," he stuttered between short breaths.

"What's the matter with him?" asked one of the children.

"He's having an asthma attack," said Miss Peterson. "Children move back and give him some room."

The children returned to their seats, their eyes fixed firmly on Luke's terrified face.

Luke was thinking of the war and the Blitz, just like Grandpa had told him. Luke was there. "Can you hear the sound of the sirens? Listen to the drone of the bombers coming closer. There's going to be an attack. Now don't panic. Just put on the gas mask like you've been taught at school..."

"But its too tight and I can't breathe, I can't..."

"Get the Headteacher," Miss Peterson shouted to Janet the class monitor, "and Bobby, bring Luke's inhaler from the cupboard at the back of the room."

Miss Peterson hurriedly removed the gas mask and the tangled straps from around Luke's head. Luke's eyes were staring and his face and hands had turned a ghastly white.

"Can I help?" asked Wayne sounding frightened.

"Get a chair," said Miss Peterson.

In just a few seconds Luke was sitting on the teacher's chair with his inhaler in his hand. After a few quick breaths Luke's colour returned to his face. He coughed and gave a weak smile as the Head teacher dashed into the room.

"Is everything all right," asked the Head teacher.

"It's okay now," said Miss Peterson quietly to Luke who looked like he'd run a full marathon. "Everything's going to be all right."

The Headteacher turned to look at Miss Peterson.

"We'd better send Luke home it's been quite an experience for him," he said.

Miss Peterson nodded her head.

"Sit here quietly for a few moments," she said to Luke. "We'll ring your mum and see if she'll come and take you home."

Wayne looked at the ground and waited for Luke to tell Miss Peterson what really happened, but Luke didn't say a word. Wayne breathed a sigh of relief. What a stupid thing to do. He'd learned his lesson well and…. he'd probably remember Miss Peterson's words for the rest of his life, "Look, but don't touch."

ALL KINDS OF CHILDREN 7

Everyone is special and has some kind of talent. You may not think that you have a talent because it is not obvious. It doesn't have to be a talent like being good at a sport or being able to sing or play an instrument. It could be a talent for being kind or caring. Whatever your talent, you should be proud of it.

Illustration available on CD ROM   ref: 36

The Talent

This is a story about four children from the same family who moved to a new school. One was good at sport, one was good at music, one was good at lessons and the other… well, she thought she was good at nothing.

The four children settled into their new school very quickly and made friends. On the second day, the children came home from school very excited.

"What have you done at school today?" asked Mum.

The one who was good at SPORT said, "I scored a hat trick at football practice today and they've asked me to play in the school team."

"My word, you are talented," said Mum.

The one who was good at MUSIC said, "I played my recorder today and they've asked me to play in assembly tomorrow."

"My word, you are talented," said Mum.

The one who was good at LESSONS said, "I got top marks in the maths test today."

"My word, you are talented," said Mum. "And what about you?" she asked the youngest child.

The little one just stood and stared.

"Well how did you do today?"

"Oh, I did nothing special," said the little one. "I haven't got any talents."

"Never mind," said Mum, "perhaps tomorrow."

But every night was the same. The children would come home from school and the three eldest would tell

Mum about what they'd done and she would smile and say well done. The little one would say nothing. By the following week the little one was really down hearted. Then Tuesday came. Everyone went into assembly as usual. The Head teacher announced that every Tuesday was a special assembly when awards would be given out to the children who had achieved something the previous week. One by one, he announced several of the children's names.

Then he said, "I have an award to give to a child with a very special talent."

He called out the name of the youngest child. Shyly, she went up to the front of the hall.

"But I haven't got a talent," she said.

"Oh yes you have," said the Head teacher.

"Who cleaned out all the paint pots last week?"

"I did," said the child.

"Who watered the plants every day?"

"I did," said the child.

"Who helped the teacher carry her books?"

"I did," said the child.

"And who helped the little girl who fell in the yard?"

"I did," said the child.

"Well, you certainly do have a talent, a talent for being helpful. There couldn't be a nicer person in the school," said the Head teacher.

"But that isn't a talent," said the little girl.

"Oh yes it is," said the Head teacher. "Listen to this poem. It will explain everything."

Have you got a talent?

I wonder what it could be,

Perhaps it's playing the recorder

Or singing perfectly.

You may be good at spelling

Write neatly with a pen,

Perhaps you can say all your tables

And always get ten out of ten.

You may bowl fast at cricket

86

Or in football score the goals,
Perhaps you're good at gymnastics
Head stands and forward rolls.
You may not think you have a talent
Because it's not there for all to see,
But perhaps you're kind and thoughtful
And that means a lot to me.

CONSEQUENCES 1

'A Heart of Stone' is a story about a boy who is unkind to people. He pays the consequences when a strange little man magically turns the boy into a stone statue. The boy learns his lesson and promises to be good in the future.

Illustration available on
CD ROM   ref: 37

A Heart of Stone

Tommy was a tall boy for his age. He was quite clever and a talented sportsman. Tommy always had lots of children to play with. They always wanted to be in his teams when he chose sides for games in the yard. They shared their crisps with him and let him borrow their cricket bats and footballs. Sometimes Tommy was kind and fun to be with. He often told jokes and made the other children laugh, but sometimes he was cruel and hurtful, especially when things didn't go his way.

At the beginning of the autumn term a new boy came to the class. He was from a different part of the country and had a strange accent. He was small for his age and very quiet. The new boy's name was Jake.

On the second day of term, Tommy decided to have some fun with the new boy just to make the other children laugh.

"Where did you come from? Outer space?" Tommy shouted.

Jake ignored him.

"Hey you! What language do you speak on your planet? Or can you not speak at all?" shouted Tommy.

Jake looked at Tommy and turned away.

At playtime the following day, Tommy decided to tease Jake again.

"Who cut your hair? Did he have his eyes shut?" said Tommy smiling.

Jake walked away feeling rather upset.

Tommy teased Jake so much that when he went to bed he cried.

"I hate that school. Tommy is so mean to me. I wish I could make him stop," he cried.

Suddenly a strange mist surrounded Jake's bed and in the twinkling of an eye, a strange little man appeared at his bedside. "What's the matter Jake? Why are you crying?" asked the little man.

Choking back the tears, Jake told him what had happened at school.

"It seems to me that you have a problem on your hands. Tommy has a heart of stone and needs to learn his lesson. Well, I'm here to help you. If he teases you again, then say these words, 'you're cruel and unkind Tommy Dixon, You really have a heart of stone.' That should do the trick."

But before Jake could say anything, the little man had disappeared. The next day was Friday. Jake set off to school with a heavy heart. At playtime he tried to avoid Tommy, but Tommy saw him in a corner of the yard and came up to him.

"Hello Ugly. How did you get such an ugly face? Perhaps your parents are Martians and you really are from outer space!" laughed Tommy loudly to attract attention.

"Stop it, stop it!" shouted Jake, But Tommy didn't take any notice of him.

"Monster Martian! Monster Munch!" shouted Tommy.

Jake turned around and just as if he were hypnotised, repeated the words the little man had told him.

"You're cruel and unkind Tommy Dixon, you really have a heart of stone."

And with a flash and a bang, Tommy Dixon turned into a statue, right in the middle of the yard!"

The children stood and stared.

Sarah and Joanne, the identical twins from the top class, saw what happened. In unison they called to the dinner ladies, "Come and look at Tommy Dixon. He's turned into a stone statue!"

Everyone crowded around and began laughing. It was the first time anyone had ever laughed at him and he was unable to tell them to stop. He was as stiff as a stone statue. Not only was his heart made of stone, but everything else too. When the bell rang for afternoon school, Tommy stayed out in the yard because he was too heavy to bring inside.

After school, Jake and the other

children went into the playground to look at Tommy the statue.

"Look!" shouted Carole, one of the girls in Tommy's class, "There are tears rolling down Tommy's cheeks. He hasn't got a heart of stone after all!"

And it was true, there were real tears falling from his stone face.

In an instant there was a flash and a bang, and before you could blink an eye, Tommy had changed back into a boy.

"I'm sorry," he said wiping the tears from his eyes. "I never realised what a cruel, heartless boy I am. Jake, I'm sorry for all the terrible things I said to you. Can you forgive me?"

"Yes of course I can," said Jake. "By the way, it's my birthday party on Saturday. Would you like to come?"

"Oh yes please," said Tommy rather timidly. "But there's just one thing. We won't be playing musical statues will we?"

"No, of course not," said Jake laughing, "It's not much fun being a statue is it!"

CONSEQUENCES 2

Percy and the Cans is a tale about a scruffy lad who didn't see any reason to keep anything clean and tidy.

However, an enterprise that ended in disaster soon taught him the error of his ways.

Poetry text available on CD ROM   ref: 38

Percy and the Cans
A Cautionary Tale

Percy was a scruffy lad
It made his parents very mad,
His bedroom it was like a tip
The rubbish would have filled a skip,
If you opened the wardrobe door
You'd find his clothes upon the floor,
And every week on washing day
His mother would be sure to say,
"What's this mark on your shirt?
It looks like blood, have you been
   hurt?

Percy you must try to be
A boy who is clean and tidy,
If you don't you'll regret the day
These very words I had to say!"
Percy didn't seem to mind
About the things that mothers find,
His lunch box it was left to rot
With things inside he had forgot,
A chicken leg, a piece of cheese
Banana skin and mouldy peas
Until one day he learned to be
In all the school the most tidy,

The teacher said, "Start saving cans,

It's for recycling you understand,

We'll take them to the big factory

It's good for the earth and makes us
money."

Well Percy just threw his cans away

Until something happened at school
one day,

He had an idea in his head

"I'll take the cans to the factory instead,

I'll get the money and spend it on me

This is business can't you see."

But unfortunately Percy fell

And along the conveyor belt he went
as well,

The cans were squashed one by one

Percy thought he was dead and gone,

But suddenly there was a cough

And a voice cried, "Switch it off!

That's not a can, can't you see

It is a boy, it's our Percy!"

In tears poor little Percy cried

"On this machine I nearly died

I've learned my lesson can't you see

I promise now I'll be tidy!"

CONSEQUENCES 3

*Most of the children we come into
contact with at school have a
reasonable standard of living.
Although children see reports on
television of what it is like in other
parts of the world, it is difficult for
them to understand what it is like to
live in a poor country where it hardly
ever rains, where there is no food and
nowhere to shelter. The poem 'Worlds
Apart', explains very simply two lives;
a child in a developed country and a
child living in the Third World. It tries
to put over the point that sometimes
we cannot help the circumstances in
which we live; nor can we alter the
consequences.*

 Poetry text available on
CD ROM   ref: 39

Worlds Apart

You and I

Are worlds apart,

I have a house

You have a box,

I have running water

You have a dried up well,

I have a plate of steaming hot food

You have an empty bowl,

I feel the rain on my cheeks

You feel the sun burn your body,

I see the green fields and golden wheat

You see your land burned to a crisp,

I see my family; my friends and they're smiling

You see your family waste away.

I have everything

You have nothing,

We're worlds apart

You and I.

Play Script
available on
CD ROM
ref: 40

CONSEQUENCES 4

This is a play for children to read or perform, requiring a few props or costumes. The story tries to explain to the children that what they do and what they say may result in them having to pay the consequence.

Mervyn the Martian

Narrator:	The place – a courtroom.
The accused:	*a ten-year-old boy.* The crime – being a pain in the neck!
Judge:	Do you Mervyn Martian, promise to tell the truth, the whole truth and nothing but the truth, so help you God?
Mervyn:	Yes I do.
Judge:	Mervyn is it true you put frogs in the swimming pool and as a result no one could go swimming for a month?
Mervyn:	Yes.
Judge:	Is it true that you ate all the buns your mother made for your brother's party and everyone else had to go without?
Mervyn:	Yes.
Judge:	And finally, is it true that you popped the school football and the match had to be cancelled?

Mervyn:	Yes.
Judge:	Now, I look to the jury for their decision. How do you find this boy?
Jury:	Guilty!
Judge:	Therefore we have no alternative but to make you pay for your crimes. You are sentenced to spend time on the planet Earth, and only when you change your ways can you return to Mars!
Mervyn:	But please your honour, don't send me there, it's the worst place in the Universe.
Judge:	I am sorry Mervyn, but we have made our decision. Your destination is a primary school in England.
Narrator:	Mervyn climbed into his space ship, tears rolling down his green cheeks.
	5 4 3 2 1 BLAST OFF! The space ship rose high above planet Mars. It touched down at …………… ………………… Primary School. Mervyn walked inside and knocked on the Headteacher's door.
Headteacher:	We've been expecting you Mervyn!
Narrator:	Mervyn was introduced to his new teacher and sat down with the other children. At first he remembered what the Martian judge had told him, but this did not last very long. At dinnertime his teacher called to him.
Teacher:	Will you help me sort out the library books Mervyn? They're all mixed up.
Mervyn:	I'm sorry; I'm going to play football.
Narrator:	As a consequence the teacher spent all dinnertime sorting out the books and didn't have time for lunch. Mervyn began playing football, but he'd never played to earthly rules before and wasn't very good.
	He decided that in order to get the ball, he'd have to kick the legs of the person who was dribbling with it. He gave the boy a big kick and then picked up the ball and threw it

over the wall.

As a consequence, the ball ran right into the path of a double-decker bus and was squashed.

The boy who had been kicked limped inside with a massive bruise on his leg.

Mervyn began to feel very hungry. He wasn't used to Earth school dinners. He looked around and noticed a little girl eating a bag of crisps. He ran over to her and took the crisps out of her hand. He ate them so quickly, half of them dropped on the playground and made the yard look very untidy. One of the older children noticed what was going on.

Child:	Mervyn, you shouldn't have done that. You stole those crisps and you've made the yard look untidy. The caretaker will not be very pleased.
Narrator:	Mervyn just pulled a face and ran off.
Mervyn:	Mind your own business you silly fool!
Narrator:	When the bell rang for the end of dinner-time Mervyn rushed straight inside without lining up. He was running so fast, he went flying into a man who had come to see the Head teacher. As a result the man fell over and had to be picked up by two dinner ladies who took him to the staff room where he could sit down and get his breath back.

The Green Policeman appears on the scene.

Green Policeman:	Do you know who I am Mervyn?
Mervyn:	Oh no! You're the Green Policeman from Mars.

Green Policeman:	And I've been watching you through my magic binoculars all day. You're a disgrace to your planet. You had better change your ways very quickly or your stay on Earth will be a long one.
Mervyn:	I'm sorry. Please forgive me and give me a second chance!
Narrator:	Mervyn behaved himself all afternoon. He worked hard in

class. He helped the teacher with the paint pots and even took a message to the Secretary. At home time he opened the door for a visitor and gave his ball to the boy he had kicked and bought some more crisps for the little girl whose bag he had stolen.

After school he walked home to his space ship feeling ashamed for all the dreadful things he had done that day. The Green policeman was waiting for him.

Green Policeman: Hello Mervyn. Perhaps you can tell me what you have learned today from the Earthlings?

Mervyn: I really learned a lot today. I learned how to behave and consider other people. And it's funny, when you do this, people around you seem to treat you differently – in a much nicer way really. Thank you for giving me a second chance.

Green Policeman: You can go home now Mervyn, but let this be a lesson to you.

Narrator: Mervyn climbed into his space ship. 5 4 3 2 1 BLAST OFF!

Green Policeman: I think that Mervyn has learned a great deal today. I hope you have too. Remember if ever you do something wrong, you may have to pay the consequences – and that may be a sentence on Mars. And you wouldn't like that would you?

CONSEQUENCES 5

The poem, 'Just One Tree', tries to explain the ripple in the pond effect. Children should be aware of the importance of the forests and realise that the cutting down of just one tree can have dire consequences. The poem puts forward the points of view of the timber company and the animals that live in the forest.

Poetry text available on
CD ROM   ref: 41

Just One Tree

(The lumberjack)
"Now don't you worry,
it's just a tree,"
said the lumberjack
from the timber company.
"We need the wood,
why should you care?
There's plenty more forest
For you out there."

(The animals)

"But it's our forest,"
the animals agreed,
"You're doing it for money
it's just pure greed!"
"What about the consequences?"
said the silver back gorilla,
"You seem like an animal killer.
If you chop down this tree

What will happen to the mouse?
For deep amongst the roots
He has built his house.
And what about the monkeys?
Leaves are their meal,
the elephants needs lots of greens
how do you think they'll feel?
The parrot needs the tree also.

The snakes and butterflies too,
The spiders living on the bark,
Oh what are they to do?
In time one species will die out
and so will the others too,
the food chain will be broken
then what are we to do?

So spare a thought for this dear tree
Although it is just one
For if you chop down all of them
soon the forests will be gone!"

ANGER 1

It is so easy to lose your temper when somebody is continually cruel to you and says unkind words. Children should be encouraged to 'turn the other cheek' and not retaliate. 'Little Brown Bull' is about a bull that is continually reprimanded by the farmer's wife. He associates her RED scarf with anger and causes havoc at the carnival when he loses his temper for the last time.

Illustration available on
CD ROM   ref: 42

Little Brown Bull

Not far from the Mediterranean Sea, on the Spanish mainland, a bull had been born in farmer Pedro's field.

"What shall we call it?" asked Pedro, looking at the young bull. His son Jose climbed up on the gate. He looked in the field, at the tiny bull with its mother.

"Let's call him Kicker," said Jose.

"Kicker! That's a strange name for a bull," said his father. "Why ever do you want to call him that?"

"Well, yesterday he tried to get out of the pen and when his mother reprimanded him, he kicked up an almighty fuss. You should have seen the pen. It was like a dust bowl."

95

"Well it is your little brown bull."

So the little brown bull was called, 'Kicker', and he became Jose's pet. All through the spring, Jose spent everyday at the pen teaching Kicker how to behave.

"You must learn to be a well behaved bull and then I can enter you in the show at the carnival this summer."

Kicker looked at Jose adoringly.

"I will do my best," thought Kicker.

Kicker was a good little bull, but occasionally he lost his temper. There was one person who could really make him do this. That person was Lolita, the farmer's wife. She didn't like bulls and she certainly didn't seem to like Kicker much. She was always shouting at him.

"Don't do this! Don't do that! Get out of the garden! Don't trample on the flowers!" she would shout.

Kicker didn't even need to hear her voice to know that she was coming, because she always wore a RED scarf, the brightest RED scarf you have ever seen.

"She makes me mad," thought Kicker; "I'd like to butt her over the fence."

But of course he never did.

Although Lolita didn't like Kicker, the local children liked him very much. They would stand on the fence and call to him.

"Aren't you a lovely bull," or "I wish you were mine."

Kicker enjoyed all the attention and would strut around the pen as if he were in an arena. Within weeks, Kicker was one of the best-trained bulls you have ever seen.

"I'm going to be so proud of you when we walk through the town to the arena," said Jose. "You will be on your best behaviour won't you?" he asked Kicker.

"Of course I will," thought Kicker, "As long as Lolita doesn't walk beside me. She'll only shout at me and tell me I'm doing something wrong."

On the morning of the show, Jose was up at the crack of dawn. He dressed in a new suit that his mother had made him and on his head he wore a hard black hat. Kicker had been scrubbed and washed down the day before; his hard, brown skin was bright and shiny.

"You look the best baby bull in the whole of Spain," said Jose proudly. Suddenly Kicker and Jose heard a scream.

Then they saw Lolita rushing across the field shaking her fist.

"Oh no," thought Kicker, "What have I done now?"

"You horrible little bull," she shouted, "just look what you have done to my dress."

She held out a dusty piece of material

with hoof prints on it. Kicker waited for Jose to give an explanation.

"I'm sorry Mother," said Jose apologetically. "We were playing hide and seek and I hid behind the washing line. Kicker accidentally knocked the pole over and all the washing fell off. He didn't mean to do it."

Lolita shook her fist and bellowed, "That bull, I hate that bull. He's a good for nothing show off. He ought to be taken down to the market and used for dog meat!"

"What?" thought Kicker, "Dog meat!"

Kicker saw RED. He lifted his head and began to snort. He kicked up the dust with one of his front hooves, ready to charge at Lolita. Jose grabbed his tail just in time.

"Don't get angry, Kicker," he said, "otherwise Mother will not take us to the show."

Kicker managed to calm himself but he snorted as Lolita stomped off back to the house, her RED scarf flying in the breeze.

Jose's family drove into town. The streets were lined with people waving and cheering. The carnival began with the band marching up the main street followed by decorated floats. Then, last of all came the bulls. Bulls of all shapes and sizes, but none like Kicker. He walked proudly by Jose's side. Jose smiled at Kicker.

"You're my best friend," thought Kicker, "I'll be on my best behaviour for you today and maybe win the cup."

The procession made its way to the arena. One by one, the commentator called the baby bulls into the arena. The crowd cheered and clapped their hands as the young bulls trotted around the arena with their proud owners. The town Mayor walked into the arena followed by his wife. He looked at all the entrants. He coughed and sighed, chortled and then finally smiled at Kicker. Meanwhile one of the bulls becoming impatient kicked up some dust with his hooves. The Mayoress sneezed.

"Have my handkerchief dear," said the Mayor.

Out of his pocket, the Mayor pulled

out a large RED handkerchief

"Oh no, not now," thought Jose, "Not a RED one!"

But Kicker had seen it, and associating the red colour with the unkind Lolita, Kicker's eyes lit up in anger. He shook his head with fury and kicked up his heels. Without even realising what he was doing, he headed straight for the Mayoress.

"Help!" she cried.

Then there was turmoil. The young bulls and their owners ran in all directions while Kicker went on the rampage.

"Come back here!" shouted Jose.

But Kicker didn't listen. He was in a rage. He ran across the arena chasing anything that moved. He ran down the main street and knocked over a flower seller's stall. He pierced an old lady's hat with his horns and ran down the street with the straw hat firmly balanced on the end of them. Kicker didn't stop running until he had reached the safety of his own pen. He lay down exhausted.

Not long after, the family returned. Kicker hid his head in the straw. "How could you lose your temper like that?" asked Pedro.

"I don't know," thought Kicker, "I just saw RED."

Kicker lifted his head slowly in shame. He could see Jose sitting at the gate with his head in his hands. Tears were trickling down Jose's chin onto his best suit.

"I'm sorry Jose," Kicker thought.

Then Lolita put her head over the fence. Kicker was frightened. He thought she was going to shout at him again. But this time her voice was different. She spoke kindly to him.

"I think it was partly my fault Kicker," she said. "I've said lots of unkind things. It's no wonder you associated my red scarf with anger. I promise never to shout at you again, as long as you promise never to get angry."

"Yes, I promise never to get angry again," thought Kicker, "even if I do see RED!"

Lolita patted Kicker's head and smiled. Kicker licked her hand in return. Then Kicker ran over to Jose and nuzzled him with his nose, making his tears stop and finally bringing a smile to his tear stained face.

So, perhaps, now you know why bulls get angry when they see red. If ever you go to Spain and see a bull, be sure you're not wearing a RED scarf!

N.B. This is a story and is not meant to be factually correct. Bulls are colour blind.

ANGER 2

When we lose our tempers we are often sorry afterwards. Sometimes we are fortunate enough to be given the chance to say sorry. However, we must learn to think before we lose our tempers, because we may not always have the opportunity to say sorry and may have to live with guilt for the remainder of our lives.

 Poetry text available on CD ROM   ref: 43

Regrets

I'll never forget you
You were my Grandma
The only one I had,
We were good friends
You and I,
Saturdays were my favourites
For I spent them with you,
We baked in the kitchen,
We listened to your old records
And looked at photo albums,
But now you're in Heaven
With Grandpa.

I'll never forget the last time
I came to your house,
You always used to leave

My pocket money on a plate.
But that day it wasn't there,
I got angry and shouted
Because I wouldn't be able
To buy my favourite comic,
I didn't really notice
The pain in your face
As you sat in the arm chair
Saying you were sorry.

I didn't notice
Your feeble, old legs
And your stiff, bent back.
I stormed out of the house
Shouting….
And that night
The phone never stopped ringing,
For you had collapsed
And were taken into hospital,
And by then
It was too late,
Too late to say sorry.

ANGER 3

Sometimes we act in anger without thinking what the consequences will be. The story, 'Why The Blackbird Sings', is about a blackbird who gets angry and blames a cuckoo for the

99

disappearance of his eggs. The result is fatal and because of this, the blackbird tells his chicks the story in the hope that they won't make the same error.

Illustration available on
CD ROM   ref: 44

Why the Blackbird Sings

Mr and Mrs Blackbird lived in an oak wood. Every evening they would sit in their nest and tell their chicks stories from long ago.

"Why do you have such a lovely voice?" asked one of the chicks.

"It is a sad story," said Mrs Blackbird, "One I don't think that your father would like to tell you."

"But I shall tell you the story," said Mr Blackbird, "It is important," he said with a tear in his eye.

Mrs Blackbird settled the two chicks into the nest and Mr Blackbird told the story.

"In the spring of last year, we decided to build a nest in which to have our chicks. We chose a delightful spot in a privet hedge near the stream. We collected grass, roots and bits of leaves and, in March of that year Mrs Blackbird laid five eggs. They were a beautiful blue with brown spots on them. I was so proud of her. They would be lovely chicks like their mother.

Your mother sat happily on the nest while I went to tell the woodland folk our news. I flew to a high branch and puffed out my shiny black feathers. Although I couldn't sing very well, I whistled cheerfully and told the woodland folk our news.

Just a few days later, I received some bad news from the wood pigeon. He told me that my mother was ill and she wished to have me by her side before she died. Your mother wanted to go too, but we had no one to look after the eggs."

"What did you do then, father?" asked one of the chicks.

"I asked our cousins the thrushes, but they were all busy sitting on their own eggs. I was so desperate, I flew onto the branch and called out to the other birds. But all the other thrushes and blackbirds were too busy sitting on their own eggs. Then I heard a voice below me. It was Mrs Cuckoo. She said that she would look after our eggs. I looked at her suspiciously. I had heard so many tales about her. Her family had been known to steal other birds' nests. Would she steal our eggs? Could she be trusted? I just didn't know. But your mother was desperate for us both to go and so there was no alternative. We left the eggs in Mrs Cuckoo's care."

"But what happened when you

oak tree. I shouted, "You wicked, wicked cuckoo. How could you do such a dreadful thing?"

"Then I noticed something under the privet bush nearby. I looked closely and saw the feathered remains of a magpie. At that moment, Mrs Blackbird came flying down. She said she had found two of the eggs under the privet hedge and they had hatched. She said that Mrs Cuckoo had kept them from harm.

"What had happened Dad?" asked the smallest chick sleepily.

"During the night, Mr Magpie had come to our nest in order to steal our eggs. Mrs Cuckoo had fought him off and had been injured in the process. But in my rage, I acted without thinking and blamed Mrs Cuckoo. It was a terrible mistake and I will never forgive myself. I buried Mrs Cuckoo at the bottom of the tree. In my sadness I sang a mournful tune, to tell the other birds what I had done. Since that day I have sung every morning for my lost friend Mrs. Cuckoo."

"But what does all this mean?" asked the youngest chick.

"I am trying to tell you that it is unwise to lose your temper unless you have a very good reason to do so," Mr Blackbird said sadly. "You never know what the consequences will be!"

returned?" asked the biggest chick.

"We flew up to the nest and to our utmost horror saw that two of the eggs had disappeared and the rest were broken. Although I am usually a calm, kindhearted bird, I flew into a rage. I wondered what that wicked cuckoo had done to our precious eggs. I knew that I shouldn't have trusted her. I had never felt so angry. Then I heard a muffled sound below me. I flew down to the forest floor and there was Mrs Cuckoo. Her feathers were ruffled and her tail feather broken. Without a moment's hesitation, I flew at her and beat her with my wings until she lay still on a pile of leaves beneath the

ANGER 4

Sometimes we get angry because of the things that people say and do. We shout and lash out at the person who has made us angry. Before we lose our temper, we should stop and think before we act. Occasionally though, we have a right to be angry. If we see bullying, or someone hurting someone or doing things they shouldn't do, then we should respond. Even Jesus got angry sometimes and the story that tells us of this, is the one about the moneychangers in the temple, which we can find in the Bible. Mark 11

Jesus and the Money Changers

Narrator:	Jesus had gone to Jerusalem because it was the time of the Passover. He decided to go to the temple where he could pray quietly. When he got near to the temple, he couldn't believe his eyes. Jesus could see a crowd of people pushing and shouting in the courtyard outside the doorway to the temple.
Jesus:	What's happening? What are you doing?
Person 1:	We are shopping round for the best deal. Did you not know that once a year we have to pay the temple tax but we are not allowed to use our own country's currency. We have to exchange our money for the special temple coins.
Person 2:	Not only that, the traders charge us extra each time we buy the temple coins. They are getting rich off the poor people of this and surrounding countries.
Person 3:	And I was charged even more, just because I didn't have the correct coins. The man charged me for giving me my change. They really are making a lot of money out of this situation.
Person 2:	I've even heard that all of these traders are relatives of Annas, the chief priest.
Jesus:	Let me pass. Let me see for myself what is going on.
Narrator:	Jesus pushed past everyone and went further inside the

temple courtyard. It looked just like a market place.

Jesus:	This is my Father's house. It is supposed to be a house of prayer. What are you all doing here?
Dealer 1:	We're selling our birds for the people to use as sacrifices in the temple. I've brought many birds. I think I'll get some good deals today.
Jesus:	You shouldn't be here. This is not a market place.
Dealer 2:	Look, if you don't want to buy anything get out of the way. I'm trying to sell my doves.
Narrator:	Jesus was pushed out of the way. In disbelief he watched the traders selling their birds.
Dealer 3:	Doves for-sale, perfect unmarked condition. You can't buy birds like these in the town.
Dealer 4:	Only these perfect looking doves are allowed in the temple and they are excellent value at only twice the normal price.
Narrator:	Jesus couldn't believe his eyes. He flew into a rage. Never had anyone seen Jesus in such a temper. He made a whip out of cords and lashed out at the traders around him.
Jesus:	Get out of here! This is a place of prayer. You are treating this temple like a market place!
Narrator:	Jesus upset the moneychangers' tables. The coins flew all over the temple floor.
Money Changer:	Hey, what's going on?
Jesus:	You must not do this!
Narrator:	The moneychangers picked up their money and ran off. Then Jesus went over to the dealers selling doves for sacrifice. He held up his fist and shouted.
Jesus:	Take your birds and get out of here now.
Cattle seller:	But why? We're only trying to make an honest living!
Jesus:	You stupid, stupid man. You have made this sacred temple into a den of thieves. Leave now!
Narrator:	The traders took their animals and left quickly. They could

see that Jesus was very angry. Jesus knew that the traders would be displeased with him, but this did not frighten him or stop him from doing what he believed was right.

Narrator   Occasionally we have good reason to be angry. If this reason is just, we have a right to do something about it. This story shows us, that there is a right time and place for losing our temper, but it is not something that we should ever be pleased about or brag about and we should never lose our temper for selfish reasons.

HONESTY 1

Sometimes children are forced into a situation where they tell a lie so as not to appear different from the rest of the crowd. Children should be encouraged to tell the truth and not feel pressurised by others. The problem of telling one little white lie is that it often leads to another one being told and yet another, until the person ends up telling so many lies it may put them in a more difficult position than they were in at first.

 Poetry text available on CD ROM   ref: 46

The Big Lie

The children they were talking

One said, "Have you got a pet?"

Most of the children nodded

But poor Gillian got upset.

"What's the matter Gillian?

You look like you're going to cry!"

Then Gillian not wanting to be different,

Decided to tell a big lie,

She said, "I am so lucky really

I've got a budgie called Bill, he can talk

And I've got a handsome Siamese cat

And a sheep dog that I can take for a walk,

Only very recently

My mum went to the shop,

She bought me a pure white cockatoo

The squawking never stops!

And you won't believe it

For going home from school,

My dad took the car to be mended

So he took me home on a mule.

Well I suppose that's really nothing

As to what happened yesterday

We found a crocodile down by our pond

104

I wonder what the neighbours will
  say?

Last night we were woken by noises

Coming from up in the tree

So my dad caught the villain with a
  big net

It was a baby chimpanzee."

"So why are you so upset then Gillian?

You've got more pets than the zoo

Perhaps we could come and visit

That's if you'd like us to?"

"It's not so convenient," said Gillian,

"The builders are coming today

They're building a pool for the animals

And a patio where they can play!"

HONESTY 2

*Most people at sometime or other tell
lies. Often there are no repercussions
but sometimes there can be. The story,
'The Birthday Fishing Trip' tells us
about a boy who tells a lie in order to
get his own way. The consequence is
disastrous when his best friend is hurt
in an accident. A year later, he reflects
on the incident and realises how just
one lie can lead to hurting the person
you love the most.*

Illustration available on
CD ROM   ref: 47

The Birthday Fishing Trip

It was Andrew's eleventh birthday.
He ran downstairs and into the kitchen.

"Happy Birthday Son," said his mother
giving him a big hug. "I know it's
Saturday but your dad is having to
work overtime, so he left your presents
on the table. He said that he'd take
you fishing later if you wanted to."

Andrew began opening the presents;
a new cycle helmet and a brand new
fishing basket. A fishing basket!
Thoughts began to fill his head but
ignoring them as best he could, he
forced a smile and said, "Thanks mum,
they're great presents."

Then he opened the cards one by one.
The last envelope was small and pink.
He tore it open and read the words out
loud.

"To Andrew, Happy Birthday, love
Beth."

Then he felt the tears come to his eyes.
He hastily ran upstairs to his room and
flung himself down on the bed wishing
the tears would go away.

"My best friend," he whimpered. "If
only I hadn't told that lie."

He conjured up a picture of Beth, now
confined to a wheel chair for the rest
of her life, paralysed from the waist
down. He remembered how they'd
been such good friends. They'd grown
up together in the same street, went to

the same school and were even in the same class. He liked her a lot. She was such good fun.

Then the memories came flooding back of that terrible day; the day when he told that dreadful lie. It was his tenth birthday and Dad had bought him a fishing rod. He remembered the day vividly and now he could see the fishing rod out of the corner of his eye leaning up against the wardrobe door, looking as good as new.

His dad had promised to take him and Beth fishing to the disused quarry after school. Andrew was so excited about it. At school he couldn't concentrate on his lessons and was relieved when the bell rang at home time. He ran all the way home with a massive grin on his face. When he got home his mother told him the bad news.

"There are road works on the motorway and your dad's going to be late," his mum said apologetically.

Andrew asked his mum if he and Beth could go without him.

"No, I'm sorry Son," said his mother sensibly, "but you know your dad's rule. You're always to be accompanied by an adult when you go to the quarry. It's very dangerous you know. The water's deep and the banks are very slippery."

Andrew went into the lounge and switched on the television. He was really annoyed. Half an hour later he heard his mother shout,

"I'm just going to the shop to get some milk. I won't be long," she said. "We'll blow out the candles on your cake when I get back."

After a few minutes an idea came into Andrew's head. He ran upstairs and collected his rod and all the equipment he might need.

"Where are you going?" asked Carole.

"I'm going fishing with Beth," he said. "Tell mum that Beth's dad is taking us."

"But isn't Beth's dad on a late shift at the factory tonight?" queried his little sister.

"Well, tell a lie for once," answered Andrew angrily. "We'll be back at nine o'clock before it gets dark. No one need ever know."

"I'm not sure whether I can do that. It's telling lies," said Carole rather frightened.

"Oh please, Carole, I've been so excited about this trip all day. It is my birthday. After all, it's only a little fib," said Andrew pleading.

"Okay, just this once," said Carole looking down at her feet.

"See you later then," said Andrew running out of the back door.

Andrew arrived at the meeting place on the stroke of six.

"Where's your dad?" asked Beth.

"He couldn't come," replied Andrew, "but he said that it's okay for us to go together."

Andrew and Beth made their way up Crag Lane and then onto the moors. In just half an hour they reached the quarry. There was nobody else there.

"Great!" shouted Andrew, "the whole quarry to ourselves."

They set up their rods with bait and cast their lines out over the deep, blue water. Andrew and Beth chatted and told each other some new jokes they had heard at school that day. The time soon passed. The shadows across the lake became longer and a cold breeze filled the evening air.

"I think we'd better be going," said Beth. "It's almost half past eight. If we rush, we'll just get back for nine o'clock."

"Oh let's not go yet, I haven't caught anything yet. Just a few more minutes, go on, please," moaned Andrew.

Beth sat down on the bank and carried on fishing. Andrew decided that the reason for him not catching any fish was due to the bait. He leaned over and put his

hand in the tub of maggots but slipped. Quickly he reached out for the nearest thing to him. He grabbed Beth's arm. By now the grass was wet with dew and she slid off the edge of the bank and into the water. Somehow, Andrew managed to stay on the bank.

Beth floundered about in the water calling out to Andrew. He couldn't find anything to reach her with so he took off his coat and shoes and waded in. Beth was just going under for the third time. He reached out and pulled her to the side.

"My back!" she screamed, "Don't touch me!"

In panic, Andrew's only concern was to get her on dry land. Her screams echoed around the quarry, as he dragged her onto the grass.

"I'll go and get help," he shouted.

Andrew ran like the wind. He had just reached Crag Lane when he heard

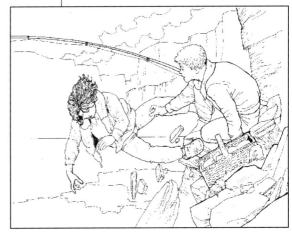

107

voices and saw some figures walking briskly towards him.

"Andrew what's happened lad?"

It was his father. Beth's dad was with him too.

As they ran up onto the moors, Andrew explained what had happened. Within minutes an ambulance could be seen racing up Crag Lane, its siren wailing. Two men with stretchers carried Beth to the ambulance and then the doors were firmly closed.

Eric sat up sharply. It was a year ago to this very day when Beth had been carried screaming to the ambulance and it was his fault entirely. He put his hands to his face and cried. He cried the tears he had never shed all that time ago. Just one lie, one small lie. How could he ever forgive himself? He pulled a handkerchief out of his pocket, blew his nose and ran downstairs.

"I'm going to Beth's," he said to his mother. "I've bought her a new computer game. I thought we could try it out."

"But it's your birthday Andrew, I thought you were going fishing with your dad," said his mother, concerned.

"No, I want to spend the day with Beth. She needs me," replied Andrew, fighting back the tears.

Andrew ran upstairs. He picked up the new fishing rod and put it in the wardrobe.

"Maybe next year," he said tearfully, closing the wardrobe door. "Maybe next year!"

Play Script
available on
CD ROM
ref: 48

HONESTY 3

A difficult concept for children to understand is that of being honest to yourself. Sometimes, a situation may arise when you are questioned about your beliefs and the easy way out would be to be untrue to yourself and agree with the majority. A situation like that could occur at school where a child realises he has different opinions from the other children but is afraid to voice them for fear of reprisals. A strong person would be brave enough to stick to their guns whatever the consequences. Daniel ch.6

Daniel in the Lions' Den

Narrator: A long time ago in the Kingdom of Babylon, there lived a man. His name was Daniel. He was a kind, truthful man, respected by others. A new king came to the throne and his name was Darius. He liked Daniel and gave him a special job. King Darius soon noticed how good and wise Daniel was and decided to give him a better job. The princes in the palace grew jealous of Daniel. They knew that Darius would not have anything bad said of Daniel, so they decided to plot against Daniel in order to get rid of him.

Youngest Prince: How can we get rid of Daniel?

Eldest Prince: We will have to find fault with him.

Youngest Prince: But he doesn't seem to have any faults.

Eldest Prince: Ah, but he does have a fault.

Youngest Prince: What's that?

Eldest Prince: He does not pray to our idols. He worships just one God. So that's how we can get rid of him.

Narrator: They thought of a plan and went to speak with the king.

Eldest Prince: I think there should be a law about worship.

King: What do you mean?

Eldest Prince: I think that if any man is seen praying to any god or man other than you, he should be thrown to the lions.

King: That seems like a good idea but do all the other princes agree?

Princes: Yes we do.

Narrator: So the king signed the agreement there and then without realising that the law could not be changed. Daniel soon heard about the new law. He could have lied to himself and changed his beliefs in order to save his life, but he did not. He continued to pray quite openly for all his enemies to see. Immediately, the princes went smiling to the king.

Eldest Prince:	We caught Daniel praying to his God and as you know, it is against the law.
Narrator:	The king was angry with himself for having signed the agreement. He knew that the princes had tricked him and that there was no way in which he could save his good friend Daniel from being thrown to the lions.
King:	Bring Daniel to me.
Narrator:	Daniel was brought to the palace and taken before the king.
King:	Is it true that you have continued praying to your God?
Daniel:	Yes it is true. If I am honest with myself I can say quite definitely that I have been praying to my own true God.
King:	Well then you must be thrown to the lions. But I will give you a chance to change your mind and if you do so I will let you go. Is it true you have been praying to your own God?
Daniel:	Yes, it is true. I will never deny my belief whatever the consequences.
King:	Then you are sentenced to the lions!
Narrator:	The king was very upset. He hoped that Daniel would have changed his mind. Daniel was taken to the lions' den and thrown inside. The king spent the evening mourning the loss of his good friend; he would not eat and sent away the minstrels who came to play for him. But the princes were extremely happy and smiled to themselves with glee.
Eldest Prince:	That's the last we'll see of him.
Youngest Prince:	I hope so.
Eldest prince:	There's nothing to worry about, believe me!
Narrator:	The next morning, the king hurried down to the lions' den expecting to see Daniel's ravaged body but at the same time hoping for a miracle. But when he rolled the heavy stone away from the entrance, the king couldn't believe his eyes. He saw Daniel standing there in front of him, without a wound or a scratch.

King:	Daniel you're alive!
Narrator:	He ran up to him and threw his arms around him.
King:	Did your God save you?
Daniel:	I believe he did. Even though they were hungry and I was trapped in here all night long, the lions did not open their mouths to hurt me.
King:	I am so pleased you are alive. Those dishonest princes tricked me and I will punish them severely. You are a good man Daniel. Today I have learned an important lesson. I have learned that you should always stand up for what you believe is right, whatever the consequences.
Daniel:	You have learned well King Darius. You too are a good man

GREED 1

Greed makes Man do terrible things. Man doesn't always realise or consider, how he is destroying his world. The needless killing of our endangered species may result in them becoming extinct. Imagine what it would be like to have the tables turned. Instead of being the hunters, man would be the hunted. After reading the poem, 'The Hunted', children might like to work out which animal they think is being discussed from the clues in the verses.

Poetry text available on
CD ROM   ref: 49

The Hunted

Imagine we're the hunted,

Imagine we're the game,

No safe place for our families

If animals we became.

Taken from our surroundings

In bags or maybe crates,

Murdered with bats or rifles

Sent to Europe or the States.

(Monkeys)
Off to the sunshine seaside resorts
To have our picture taken,
While the owners smile quite sweetly
And think of the money they're
    making.

(Parrots)
Sent to our local pet shops,
Unable to fly free
Or spread our feathers in cages
Like we did when we lived in the trees.

(Seals)
Brutally beaten with a heavy club
While we lay there on the snow,
So a lady can look nice in winter
And to cold, frosty lands she can go.

(Elephants)
Shot with a powerful rifle
Our tusks ripped out of our heads,
"This ivory makes lots of money,"
The poachers in Africa said.

(Blue whales)
Harpoons spray the water.
Fishing boats scour the sea,
So we can be served up for dinner,
A very cruel fate you'll agree.

What's it like to be hunted?
What's it like to be game?
We'll never know for we're humans
We're the only ones you can blame.

GREED 2

The poem, 'Seal', tells us about the plight of the seal, which has been incessantly hunted for its skin. It teaches us to feel compassion for animals, which have a right to live in their natural environment without the fear of poachers.

 Poetry text available on
CD ROM   ref: 50

Seals

Tears came to my eyes
As I saw this frozen land,
Being turned into a blood bath
By a club in a fisherman's hand.
A terrified, baby seal
Skinned alive by men,
As it's mother watches so helpless
In a world she can't understand.
The distraught female seal
Nursed the shattered remains,
Of her harmless lovable pup,
Who will never swim again.
On the icy, Northern wastes
The mother seal was grieving
Tears rolling down her fur
As she watched the fishermen leaving.
You see, it's not a harvest
We don't need these coats to wear,
It's barbaric and it's brutal
And it's totally unfair.

GREED 3

Play Script
available on
CD ROM
ref: 51

It is so easy to look at the negative side of people's characters and to notice their faults. However, people can be unselfish and thoughtful, and a story, which emphasises this, is 'The Widow's Mite', found in the Bible. Luke Chp. 21

The Widow's Mite

Narrator:	One day Jesus was in the temple. He had been preaching and telling everyone his good news about God. He stopped for a while and watched the people coming in and out. He saw them giving money to the temple funds.
Rich Man 1:	Hi Fred. Hi Charlie! Nice to see you. Hey, do you like my new suit? Very smart isn't it. Even Joseph didn't have a coat as colourful as this. Cost a fortune it did, never mind being as rich as I am it's not a problem really.
Narrator:	The rich man in the expensive clothes was just about to dash into the temple when he noticed the collection box for the temple funds.
Rich Man 1:	Oh yes. Oh yes. I nearly forgot. Donations for the upkeep and the work of the temple. Let's see now, I think I've got some change in here. No, is it this pocket? Ah, here it is. One, two three. There now, I think that should be quite enough!
Narrator:	After placing the three coins in the chest, the rich man smiled and went on his way pleased with himself for being so kind.

Shortly after this, a lady came along in beautiful clothes wearing expensive jewellery.

Rich Lady	Hi Ruth. Do you like my new bracelets? Solid gold they are. When I saw them in the market, well I just knew I had to have them and so I said to my husband, just look at those beautiful gold bracelets, they look as if they were made especially just for me. And of course he agreed, because he always does when I see something I just absolutely can't do with out, and so he bought them for me just there and then. Aren't I a lucky girl?

Ruth	Oh honey they're absolutely gorgeous, no girl should be without jewellery, don't you think?
Rich Lady	Of course not, I don't know how any self respecting woman could possibly be seen out without a few beads, and why not? Oh, what's this down here?
Ruth	Oh honey, that's the plate for the temple donations.
Rich Lady	Temple donations, oh yes! Now, did I bring my bag? Ah, here it is, now, did I remember my purse? It was in here this morning, is that it, no, oh here it is. Now, have I got any spare coins? One, two, three, four, five. Yes that should do.
Narrator	So the lady with the beautiful clothes and the expensive jewellery put five coins in to the collecting box and went on her way.

Shortly after another wealthy looking man came along drawing lots of attention to himself.

Rich Man 2	Morning! Morning! Good morning to you over there! Lovely day, isn't it? I'm just here to say a few prayers for the good of the world and then I'll be on my way. Now, where is the temple collecting box? I'm feeling extremely generous today, I've just heard that my business has had its best ever year and is expected to grow even more next year.
Doorman:	Here you are sir, the temple collecting box.
Rich Man 2:	Let me look in my wallet. Ah yes, here are my spare coins. In fact, I'm feeling so generous; I'll even put one of these large paper notes in the box. I bet they've not had one of those for some time.
Doorman:	Most generous sir.
Narrator:	Later that morning, the wealthy people all left the temple with their heads held high and with great big smiles on their faces. Not long after they had left, an old widow quietly walked in. She was dressed in simple clothes and it was obvious she was quite poor. Without making a scene, the old lady walked up to the temple collecting box. She felt in her pocket and brought out two small coins, which she held

in her hand. Quietly, and without fuss, she dropped the coins into the chest and continued on her way.

Jesus:	Peter, Matthew, the rest of you, come over here a moment.
Peter:	What is it Jesus?
Jesus:	Did you see that old lady?
Matthew:	No, but I did see two wealthy looking men and a well dressed lady go by.
Peter:	The first man put at least three silver coins in the temple chest.
Matthew:	And the lady put five silver coins in the chest.
Jesus:	So who do you think has given most generously?
Peter:	Oh, that's easy to answer. I saw another man gave silver coins and a large note.
Jesus:	Well listen to what I have to tell you. The poor old woman that threw two coins into the chest was the most generous.
Matthew:	Why was that Lord? Surely the others gave much more.
Jesus:	The wealthy people only gave the money they could easily spare from their great riches. The widow, despite being very poor, gave everything she had to live on. This makes her very special and the most generous of anyone here today.
Narrator:	The disciples looked at Jesus and nodded in agreement. Her gift was certainly the most worthy.

GREED 4

Young children often think that greed is only associated with food, but there are other forms of greed. The story, 'Grandpa,' is about an old man who has lost everything because of his greedy ways. However, in the story he is given a second chance.

 Illustration available on CD ROM   ref: 52

Grandpa

Mr Tucker sits in the armchair by the fire. He stares at the dancing flames with a haunted look on his face. Warily he looks around the room at the few remaining pensioners. It is Sunday afternoon and most of them have gone out with their families to the seaside or to have a roast dinner at their relative's houses. Some of those who can't walk very well entertain their families in the home. He can see the old people smiling as they watch their grandchildren laugh and play little games. Mr Tucker sighs. He shuts his eyes and thinks of days gone by.

He remembers when he was a toddler. He never gave his mother a minute. He never left her side, pulling on her skirt and screaming for attention. Then, he was greedy for time.

He remembers when he was a boy at school. He always wanted what other people had; a new bike, a new cricket bat, trips to the seaside. He was never satisfied. Then he was greedy for possessions.

He remembers when he was a young man. He had a wonderful wife, everything a man could wish for. But he was possessive. He didn't like anyone else talking to her or smiling at her. He lost her to another man. Then, he was greedy for love.

He remembers when he got older. He had no family, no one with whom he could share his good fortune. He built up his business from nothing, but wasn't satisfied. He had to do more, whatever the cost to other firms. He carried on regardless of who was trampled under foot. Then he was greedy for money and power.

Now, he's a rich old man, but there's no one with whom he can share his good fortune. He's lost all the people he loved on the way. No one ever comes to visit. Now, on his seventieth birthday, he will expect nothing and believes no one will call. He's been a greedy man and deserves to be treated like this. But he has changed; he does care. If only he could let them know. Beginning to doze off by the fire, he feels someone tapping on his shoulder.

"Mr Tucker, there are some people to see you," says the nurse quietly in his ear.

Mr Tucker watches the door open and tears well up in his soft, brown eyes.

"Hi Dad, Happy Birthday," says William Tucker his son, shaking him by the hand,

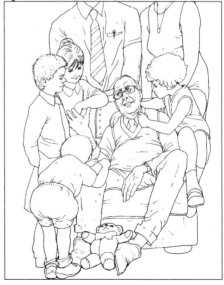

"Hello Son, it's good to see you after all this time," says Mr Tucker shakily.

"I've brought you some visitors," says his son nervously. Two small children run over to Mr Tucker. The boy thrusts a present into his wrinkled, old hands,

"Happy Birthday Grandpa," says the boy excitedly. The little girl climbs up on Mr Tucker's knee and throws her arms around him.

"I love you Grandpa," she shouts, for all the people to hear.

"I love you too," answers Grandpa, "I love you all."

GREED 5

Sometimes we are not satisfied with what we have been given. We may wish for more and take what is not ours. We should learn to know when we have had enough. The poem, 'The Greedy Piglet', tells us about a pig who always wanted more to eat. However much she ate she always wanted more than her fair share. As a consequence, something unfortunate happened to her and this taught her a valuable lesson.

 Poetry text available on CD ROM   ref: 53

The Greedy Piglet

Fatima was a piglet,
She was born in spring,
Buns and all leftover meals
She liked more than anything.

Mr Green the farmer was worried
When she began getting fatter,
To twice the size of her sisters
He wondered what was the matter.

He decided to watch what was going on
And peered from behind the gate.
The piglets quite hungry came out of the pen,
"Breakfast," they thought,
"Well that's great!"

Fatima was the first to the pig trough
Pushing the others aside,
Her sisters couldn't get near it
No matter how hard they tried.

It only took a minute
Until she'd eaten the lot.
She lifted her tail high in the air
Pleased at all she had got.

Every day this happened

Mr Green didn't know what to do.

The piglets began to get thinner

While Fatima grew and grew.

And then one morning quite early

Mr Green heard Fatima squeal,

And looking into the pigsty

Saw the piglets tucking into their meal.

Fatima was inside the pigpen
Too fat to get out through the door,
Her bottom had lodged in the opening
Her head firmly fixed on the floor.
Fatima stayed there a few days
Until she had lost enough weight,
Somehow she learned her lesson
Thank goodness it wasn't too late!

LOVE 1

The origin of St. Valentine coincides with the coming of Christianity. One belief is that St. Valentine was an Italian priest who at the time of the Roman Empire, was imprisoned for his beliefs. During his imprisonment, he restored the sight of the gaoler's daughter.

 Illustration available on CD ROM   ref: 54

St. Valentine

This story begins a long, long time ago in the far off country of Italy. It was during the period of the great Roman Empire. The story is about a boy named Valentine who was just like any other Italian boy except for one thing. When all the other boys were out climbing trees or playing at gladiators, Valentine could be found helping children who had perhaps fallen, or he could be heard talking to those who were upset about something. Valentine loved life and loved people. He was a kind, helpful boy who cared about every living thing. His mother would say, "Valentine, you're a good boy. When you become a man you'll make someone a wonderful husband."

However when Valentine grew up, he decided to devote his life to the church. Valentine became a Christian. He was dedicated to the faith and finally became a priest.

His mother said, "Valentine, are you not afraid to be a Christian? If the Romans find you, they will put you in prison and torture you."

But Valentine always had the same reply. "I love God and humanity and I will never renounce the Christian faith whatever happens!"

Not long after, Valentine was captured and put in prison by the Romans. One of the prisoners spoke to Valentine saying, "Why don't you give up believing in this God you keep telling us about and then I'm sure they will set you free!"

Valentine replied, "I will always be a Christian and love my fellow man."

The prisoner replied, "But how can you love people who hurt you? They whip you and say cruel words. Surely you must hate them?"

"I hate no man. I love everyone equally, whatever they do to me," Valentine replied.

The Roman guards were cruel, hard men. They enjoyed teasing Valentine. The gaoler in the prison was a tough man and didn't like Christians.

He said, "Hey Valentine, if this God of yours is so wonderful why doesn't he come and set you free?"

But Valentine never replied. He would merely look at the gaoler thinking how sad it must be to have such a cold heart.

Some time later, Valentine noticed that the gaoler had not been at work for several days. He called one of the Roman guards.

"Where is he?" Valentine asked.

"He's at home with his daughter who is blind. He loves her more than anything in the world. He takes her around the countryside and describes all the things she is unable to see. Without him her life would be darkness," said the guard.

"Tell him to bring her to me," said Valentine. "I think I can help."

Several days later the gaoler returned, holding his daughter's hand tightly.

"And what do you think you can do?" sneered the gaoler. "You can't even escape from the prison!"

"But I have faith and faith can move mountains. Bring her to me," replied Valentine.

Valentine looked kindly at the girl and said, "Do not be afraid for I will not hurt you."

Valentine gently touched the girl's face with his hands. "You have a good heart," he said.

The young girl lifted her head slowly. Then with the blink of an eye she turned and ran to her father.

"Daddy I can see!" she shouted.

"But how? It's impossible," said the gaoler shaking his head.

Valentine replied, "Nothing is impossible. All you need is faith. Learn to trust your fellow men and most of all learn how to love."

LOVE 2

As children grow up, they learn about relationships. If children are to become loving adults they have to learn how to forgive and accept people for what they are. The story, 'The Accident', is a modern version of 'The Good Samaritan'. It tells the story of two boys, one of whom didn't like the other. When one boy gets hurt, the other one has to make a decision whether to help him or not. Just like the story from the Bible, the boy helps the other one and they become friends. This story tries to explain that two wrongs don't make a right. The response to hate should be love, for only good things can come of love.

 Illustration available on CD ROM   ref: 55

The Accident

Everyone knew about the 'Rec', for it was a children's paradise. Adults couldn't understand what the attraction was. After all, it was just a large group of oak trees behind Joe Baynes' factory, with a somewhat dried up old stream running through it.

The person who spent most time at the 'Rec', was Tony Baynes. His dad owned the factory and for that reason Tony thought that the 'Rec' belonged to him. Tony and a group of lads had made a rope swing. It hung from a branch of an old oak tree at the top of the bank. The rope dangled over the stream. Tony constantly told the other boys how his older brother had fallen from the swing and landed in the stream. Somehow, his brother had bravely staggered home even though an X-ray later showed a fractured ankle.

One Saturday morning Tony's gang were walking to the 'Rec' when they heard voices. Quickly, getting down on all fours and sliding along the grass, they could see Rob Williams and a few other lads playing on the rope swing.

Tony jumped up and with a shout of, "Get 'em!" Tony's gang jumped up and ran towards the stream.

"Hey you!" shouted Tony, "Get off that swing, it's mine."

"Why should we? It's not yours at all!" shouted Rob Williams.

"Because if you don't, I'll come up there and throw you off!" replied Tony.

Tony's gang ran towards the group of boys. Quick as lightning, the younger boys set off at a pace through the wood. Tony could hear Rob's voice in the distance shouting back to him,

"That rope swing of yours is dangerous, anyway, it's beginning to fray!"

"Rubbish!" shouted one of Tony's gang, "It's the best rope swing around."

Tony waited until the younger boys had gone and then said, "We'll have to organise a lookout in case they come back."

"Great idea," agreed the gang.

After school on Monday there was a football practice. Tony was there in goal and Rob Williams was there too. Although Rob was only nine, he was a neat player and very fast. He'd scored lots of goals during the football season too. Taking a dive to meet a header, Rob fell headlong into the goalmouth and Tony dived on top of him pretending to stop the ball from going into the net.

"Ouch!" shouted Rob picking himself off the ground.

"Sorry," said Tony with a smile on his face, but whispering in Rob's ear, "You'd better stay away from my swing or else!"

Rob ignored the comment and slowly, with the help of two other lads, was lifted to his feet.

"I'm sorry Sir, but I think I've twisted my ankle," said Rob, "I can't put any weight on it."

The teacher ran over, "Come on lads help him inside. I'd better have a look at it. We'll finish for now, okay."

Tony looked over at his friends, "Well that should keep him away from the 'Rec' for a while," he said smiling.

For the rest of the week, Tony's gang kept watch over the 'Rec'. On Friday evening it was Tony's turn.

He'd been sitting on the bank for over an hour and none of Rob's friends had appeared. He was just about to leave when he saw a figure appear down by the stream. It was Rob.

"Hey you, I've told you not to come here!" shouted Tony at the top of his voice.

"I've brought you a peace offering," said Rob. "It's a new rope. I thought you might need it. Perhaps if I put it up for you, we could all use it. How about it?"

"No way," replied Tony. "There's nothing wrong with this one. Now clear off." Rob turned and walked away.

"What a nerve," thought Tony as he grabbed hold of the rope.

Tony took a run up and swung out over the stream. The rope seemed fine. He decided to go for a bigger swing.

"Geronimo!" he shouted as he flew out over the banking.

But Tony's weight unravelled the last strands of rope and with a ping, the rope snapped. Tony came flying down. He landed with a thud at the edge of the stream. Stunned he lay there for a few seconds. Then he felt the pain all the way up his left arm and at the back of his head.

"Help!" he shouted, "Someone help me!"

He was surprised to see a familiar figure appear in front of him. It was Rob.

"Where does it hurt?" Rob asked.

"My head and my shoulder," Tony grimaced.

Rob noticed a cut on Tony's head. Quickly he took off his tie and tied it around Tony's head. Using his sweater he made a sling for Tony's arm and lifted him onto his feet.

"We'd better get you home quickly," he said.

On Monday morning, Tony's accident was the talk of the school.

"Can you believe it?" said one boy, "Rob Williams saved Tony Baynes' life at the 'Rec'!"

"It's unbelievable," said another boy. "Tony had been really nasty to Rob and he'd even tripped him up at football practice!"

All day long, it was the topic of conversation at school.

When Rob got home from school, his mother called him into the kitchen.

"You've had a phone call. Someone called Tony said he wants you to call at his house this evening."

Rob couldn't believe it; Tony disliked him so much.

After tea Rob knocked on Tony's door. His dad answered it.

"Come in lad," he said, "We've heard a lot about you."

Tony was sitting in bed feeling rather sorry for himself.

"I'm glad you could come. I wanted to say sorry for being such a pain and to thank you for helping me," said Tony feeling ashamed.

"It was nothing," said Rob, "I would have done the same for anyone."

Tony said, "I know I shouldn't ask, but would you be my friend? Tell the other lads too. And as soon as I'm feeling better, maybe we could go down the 'Rec' together."

"Sure," said Rob, "That would be fun. But before we do, I'd better hang up the new rope. We don't want anyone getting injured do we?"

Tony smiled and held out his hand. "Friends?" he asked.

"Why not?" answered Rob and shook Tony's hand.

LOVE 3

Play Script
available on
CD ROM
ref: 56

As we grow we learn about friendship and love. We respond to people who love us, for example our family, relatives and friends. However, it is not quite so easy for us to learn how to love people whom we dislike or who have done us wrong. Christians believe 'The Sermon on the Mount' explains Jesus' message to the people on how to live your life. Part of the sermon is concerned with loving your enemy and children should be made aware of this. Matthew ch.5

The Sermon on the Mount

Narrator: Jesus was sat on a hillside talking to his friends. Passers by stopped to hear what was happening. Eventually a small crowd had gathered and so Jesus stood and began to teach. He knew some people had come to listen to him and to be healed of their diseases. Some of the people were worried and had bad thoughts inside them so Jesus climbed the mountain and talked to them from on high. He told them how they should behave and he also told them about love.

Jesus: How joyful are the down hearted for theirs is the kingdom of heaven.

Listener 1:   How can you be happy if you are down hearted? That doesn't make sense to me.

Jesus: Do you not realise that joy can come eventually, even to those that are presently poor or sad. Everyone has the ability to be happy given time.

Listener 2:   Yes, my family is poor, but that doesn't stop us enjoying the important things in life such as having friends.

Jesus: How joyful are they who mourn for they shall be comforted.

Listener 3:   Our family was very sad when father died three years ago, so sad in fact, we never thought we would laugh again. But we did. We are still sad when we think of him but we are able to be light hearted once again.

Jesus: How joyful are the humble for they shall inherit the earth.

123

Listener 4:	What does it mean to inherit the earth? Does it mean you will be enormously rich? Surely this would make anyone happy?
Jesus:	It means, happy people are not too proud to help someone in need. True happiness does not come from great wealth, it comes from giving love and receiving the love of gratitude in return. How joyful are they who hunger and thirst after what is right, for they shall be satisfied.
Listener 5:	But how are we to know what is right so that we may become satisfied?
Jesus:	Everyone knows what is right and what is wrong but only those who are satisfied by using the right words, having right thoughts and carrying out right deeds will be truly happy.
Listener 6:	So whenever we see wrong things happening we should try to put it right. Whenever we hear bad things being said, we should stand up for the truth. I see now, but there are so many things that are not right with our world.
Jesus:	How joyful are the merciful, for they shall obtain mercy.
Listener 7:	I think I know what that means. People who are prepared to forgive someone when they have wronged them, surely they are the ones who are happy. The happiness will come from the forgiving, not from doing wrong!
Jesus:	How joyful are they who are pure in heart.
Listener 8:	This means those that intend to do the right action are happy and satisfied people.
Jesus:	How joyful are the peace-makers.
Listener 9:	I get this one, this means that those who live in a peaceful manner are happy.
Jesus:	How joyful are those that are bullied for what is right, for the kingdom of heaven is theirs.
Listener 10:	Do you mean that we have to be bullied by someone before we enter such a place as heaven? That sounds very strange to me.

Jesus:	It is not as simple as that. What I am saying is if you are standing up for what you really believe to be true and the crowd try to make you do otherwise, if you have the courage to stand up against what is wrong, then you deserve a rich reward.
Narrator:	Finally, Jesus started to talk about love. He talked in a way that no one had ever thought about before.
Jesus:	You have heard people say you must love your neighbour and hate your enemy, well today, I am telling you to love your enemies.
Listener 11:	But what do you mean? How can we possibly love our enemies?
Jesus:	It is easy to love those that love you, but have you ever tried to love people that dislike you or even hate you? Anybody can love somebody that loves them. That will not make you special. But if you can love someone who hurts you, or who calls you names and even does horrible things to you, then you really are a worthy person. If everybody loved somebody who is his or her enemy, then the world would be a better place.
Narrator:	The crowd had never heard teaching like this before. They were expected to be humble, to stand up for what is right and most of all love people who did not care at all about them. They went away confused, but thinking hard. Maybe true happiness was to be found in all of these things.

LOVE 4

Families are very important. For a child, love begins at home. Even as a baby, a child learns to trust his family and this bonding results in a deep love. The love a child has for his family has a profound effect on the way he grows up and lives his life. A child should not take love for granted. He should realise the importance of giving and taking and should show his love for his family in as many ways as possible. Mother's day is a time when a child can say thank you to his/her mother for all that she has done.

125

Mum

Mum
The only one in the world
With a smiling face
And a shoulder to cry on
When life gets hard.

Mum
Who taught you to read?
While you sat on her knee,
And gave you money
To buy sweets and comics

Mum
Who changed the bed
When you were sick?
And mopped your brow
When you lay in a fever
Mum
Who took you on the bus
To Scarborough and York,
Pushed the swing in the park
And gave you bread to feed the ducks.

Mum,
Who cooked all your favourites
And even washed the dishes
When she wasn't well,
And never had the sympathy.

Mum,
To you, she is
The most special person
In the whole, wide, world.

LOVE 5

*Nearly every child has some
grandparents living, but I wonder
how much they know about them and
how often they visit them. There are
so many exciting things that children
can do in their leisure time, that
sometimes it is only as a last thought
that they visit their grandparents or
elderly neighbours. It is important for
children to think about people older
than themselves. Children can do a
great deal for old people. A short visit
to an old person's home for a chat,
to share a joke, do odd jobs or go on
errands can make an old person very
happy. The poem, 'Penalty of Age',
tells us about old people and how they
tend to be forgotten. Children should
realise that old people too, need love
and affection.*

126

Penalty of Age

Too cold to live
Too young to die,
Too old to move
Or watch passers by.
These are the elderly
Who pass us in the street,
No one seems to notice
Their painful tired old feet.
Locked up in their houses
Curtains drawn quite tight,
Huddled by the dying fire
Sometimes through the night.
So why should we ignore
What one-day we shall be,
Shivering, hungry and lonely
Pensioners, you and me.

LOVE 6

*All our lives people surround us. As
we grow, we learn about friendship
and how valuable it is. We learn to
take ups and downs, and learn how
to respect other people and their
opinions. The poem, 'Do You
Remember?' looks at a child's
memories of school. It shows how
friendships can be very special and
also last a lifetime.*

Poetry text available on
CD ROM   ref: 59

Do you Remember?

Do you remember
The day that we met?
Our first day at school,
I shall not forget.

Do you remember,
The games and the fun
Out on the playground
When our work was done?

Do you remember
Winter and snow,
Fun in the yard
When snow balls we'd throw?

Do you remember
Our trip to the sea
The ride on the donkeys
It was fun you'll agree?

Do you remember
School, the last day,
When we all went
Our separate ways?

I haven't forgotten
Although I was just ten,
For today you're as special
As you were then.

LOVE 7

Love is a difficult concept to explain. In a material world, children sometimes think that things can be bought and don't always realise that some things like love, have to be earned. The story, 'Where is love?' is about a selfish rabbit who has not learned how to give love. He goes in search of love and realises that you cannot buy it, but you have to find it inside yourself.

Illustration available on CD ROM ref: 60

Where is Love?

Flopsy Bunny was born in the spring. His mother and father looked down at him and smiled.

"What a beautiful bunny," said his mother.

"What a handsome bunny," said his father.

But Flopsy wasn't the best of babies. He cried most nights and kept his parents awake. He refused his food and threw tantrums at the slightest things. In fact he was a naughty, selfish bunny who only cared about himself. None of the other rabbits would play with him.

"Can I play?" Flopsy would shout.

"No!" replied the other rabbits.

"Why not?" demanded Flopsy in a temper.

"Because you cheat!" shouted one.

"Because you lie!" shouted another.

"Because you don't play fairly!" said yet another rabbit.

"But I don't mean to," said Flopsy beginning to get worried. "Well, when can I play?"

"When you've got some love inside you," said one of the older rabbits.

Flopsy didn't understand.

"Love? What's that? Where do I get it from? Can I buy it? Will I find it in Farmer Thomas' field?" he asked with a concerned look in his eyes. The animals looked at him and laughed.

"You are a silly bunny," said the oldest rabbit. "go and find Wise Owl. He'll tell you where to get it from."

"Right, I'll go now. See you all later," he said seriously. "By the way, would anyone else like some love?"

The other animals giggled and then carried on with their game.

Flopsy bounded off into the wood. He sat under a tree and began to scratch his ears, wondering where he could find Wise Old Owl. Then he shouted as loudly as he could, "Does anyone know where I can find Wise Old Owl?"

He heard a noise in the branch above him.

"Hey you," shouted a voice, "What's all the fuss about?"

Flopsy looked up and saw an unusual looking bird on the branch.

"I'm looking for Wise Old Owl. Do you know where I can find him?" asked Flopsy, never having seen an owl before.

"I'm Wise Old Owl and you've woken me up!" he replied.

Why are you sleeping? It's day time," said Flopsy.

"Not all animals are like you," the owl replied. "Some of us sleep during the day. Anyway what are you doing?"

"I'm looking for love. Do you know where I can get some?" Flopsy asked seriously.

"I'm afraid it's not as easy as that," replied Wise Old Owl. "Love comes from inside you. You can give it, but you can't buy it or just take it."

"Well how can I find love?" asked Flopsy.

"Let me see," said the owl. "Love is sharing and love is caring for other people. Loving is helping and being kind to other people. Love is understanding."

"Oh," said Flopsy. "It seems rather difficult to me. Perhaps I'll wait until I'm older."

"It's up to you," replied the owl, "but are you a happy bunny?"

"No, not really. I've no friends and my family don't seem to like me either," Flopsy said rather sadly.

"Well then, perhaps you ought to go and find love, but remember my words. If you want love, you must give some in return," said Wise Old Owl.

"Perhaps you're right. Thank you for the advice. Perhaps I'll see you again one day," said Flopsy confidently.

Wise Old Owl put his head under his wing and went to sleep.

Flopsy Bunny set off home. He had just reached a clearing in the wood when he saw a baby bird under a tree.

"What's the matter?" asked Flopsy

Bunny.

"I've fallen out of the nest and I can't get back. Will you help me?" said the frightened bird.

Flopsy was just about to say, "No," when he remembered what Wise Old Owl had said about love. The owl had told him that love was about sharing.

"Yes of course you can have some," said Flopsy

The field mouse sat down with him and together they ate until their tummies were completely full.

"Thanks for the meal," said the field mouse and scampered off. Flopsy smiled a large, toothy grin. "I like sharing," he thought and then went on his way.

Some time later, as Flopsy was jumping down the lane quite happily, he could hear crying from under the hedge. He ran to where the sobbing was coming from. Underneath the hedge was a toad.

"Hello," said the toad timidly. "Will you play with me?"

Flopsy was just about to say, "No," thinking what an ugly toad he was, when he remembered the Wise Old Owl's words.

"Oh yes," he thought. "Love is about being friends and being kind and caring to other animals."

"Yes of course I'll play with you," said Flopsy.

Together, the toad and the rabbit played 'Olympics'. They jumped over tree trunks and across the stream backwards and forwards until they were too tired to jump any more.

"That was fun," said Flopsy Bunny, "We must do it again sometime."

"Thank you friend," said Toad, "I had a lovely time."

Flopsy smiled a large toothy grin and ran home.

"Hi Mum," he said jumping across the kitchen floor. "Can I help you make dinner?"

"Oh, that would be nice," said his mother somewhat surprised.

After lunch, Flopsy was just about to go out to play, when his mother called to him.

"Flopsy, would you look after baby Sarah this afternoon? I've got an errand to do."

Flopsy was just about to say, "No," when he remembered the owl's words.

"Love is about your family and showing them how much you care."

"Yes of course I will," replied Flopsy. Flopsy looked after his baby sister all afternoon. He didn't realise they could have so much fun together.

"I like you big brother," said Sarah. Flopsy smiled a large toothy grin.

"I like you too," he replied.

When the moon came out Flopsy and his sister went to bed. During the night a visitor came.

"Wake up," whispered the visitor.

Flopsy sat up in bed. It was Wise Old Owl who had come to visit. "Well, have you found love?" asked the owl.

"I think I have," said Flopsy, "and it makes me feel really good inside."

"I'm glad," said the owl, "but don't ever lose it will you?"

"No, now I've found it, I'll keep it forever," said Flopsy, and gave owl a large toothy grin.

LOVE 8

As children grow, they realise the importance of love. As an extension of family love, most children enjoy having pets. They can give love to their pets, and in looking after them and growing up with them, will feel the joys and sadness associated with life and it's natural progression. The poem, 'Candy' portrays the love for 'man's best friend', his dog. It teaches children about love and how to come to terms with death, not as a sad ending, but of experiences shared, the good times and bad, and memories that will never fade.

Poetry text available on
CD ROM   ref: 61

Candy

Candy was my dog
And now she is dead.
I don't think
I'll ever smile again,
For she was so special
The best friend I ever had,
And now she's gone
Our big house will be empty
When I come home at night.
For there'll be no greeting,

No jumping or licking,
Just a huge empty space,
In that corner of the room,
Where my husband lay her down
After the collision with the car.
No cuts or scratches
And no broken bones,
No yelps and whines,
Just still and lifeless.

And I held her
And pleaded with her,
"Candy, don't die!"
But the kiss of life
Just didn't work,
So we carried her quickly
Out to the van,
And the vet said,
"I'm afraid she will not survive!"

And life carries on,
But it won't be the same.
No walks in the fields
Or games in the garden,
No bones on a Friday
Or dips in the cow trough,
No cuddles on our laps
Or trips to the seaside,
Just emptiness.

LOVE 9

As children grow, they learn about the value of life. They begin to realise that life is special and that quality of life is just as important for an animal as it is for a human being. In these times, children hear so much about cruelty to animals. It is important that they realise that animals have every right to live in the surroundings and environment they are accustomed to. The poem, 'Elephant Dawn', sheds light on the fact that animals do have rights. So many of them are being killed for human wants – clothes, shoes, jewellery and ornaments. If we really love our world and don't wish to see so many species become endangered, then it is up to us to do something about it

 Poetry text available on CD ROM   ref: 62

Elephant Dawn

A ruby, red sun
Lifts its weary head
Over Kilimanjaro.
On the vast, green plain
A herd of elephants
Is bathing
Down at the water hole.
A family group
With trunks swaying,
The water so refreshing
On dusty, grey backs,
This is their territory
Their only freedom.
But gun fire
Disturbs the tranquil scene.
Men in khaki
Appear in trucks,
A dust trail behind them
Weaving along the plain
Like a hideous snake.
They're here for the kill
White ivory, dollar signs
In their bloodthirsty eyes.
The ruby, red sun
Bows its shameful, head
Behind Kilimanjaro
As vultures fly excitedly

Over fresh, new prey.
This magnificent creature
Left to rot,
Its blood stained head
A precious reminder,
To its young calf,
Who in fear and trembling
Nuzzles the still, warm body
Of its dead mother.